THE LEGEND OF
BO SCHEMBECHLER

THE LEGEND OF
BO SCHEMBECHLER

How an Unknown Buckeye Became the
Winningest Coach in Michigan Football History

BARRY GALLAGHER

MILL CITY PRESS

Mill City Press, Inc.
2301 Lucien Way #415
Maitland, FL 32751
407.339.4217
www.millcitypress.net

Printed in the United States of America

ISBN-13: 9781545638491

TABLE OF CONTENTS

DEDICATION

THIS BOOK IS dedicated to the memory of the winningest coach in the history of the winningest program in college football history. Bo Schembechler came to Ann Arbor as a relatively unknown coach. He left as a legend. Even though he coached at Miami of Ohio for six seasons, Bo is linked to Michigan Football forever! He put Wolverine Football back on the "national" map and positioned it to stay there for a very, very, long time. Thanks to Glenn Edward "Bo" Schembechler for his tireless efforts to make Michigan Football "the leaders and the best" again! A portion of the proceeds from the sale of this book will be donated to the Glenn Edward "Bo" Schembechler Scholarship Program at The University of Michigan in honor of Coach Schembechler. Go Blue!

NOTE

ALL REFERENCES TO ohio state, columbus (as in ohio) and buckeyes in this book begin with a lower-case letter. This is not a error in grammar or a typographical mistake. It is simply an intentional act performed by a Die Hard Maize and Blue Football Fan. Woody Hayes did not consider it proper to refer to The University of Michigan, the Wolverines or anything associated with the Great State of Michigan with other than "the team up north." So, it is only fitting to ignore the conventions of good spelling and capitalization and use all lower-case letters when talking about all things near and dear to Woody's heart. Out of respect for his mother and father, who named him, I do use proper spelling and capitalization in my references to their son, Woodrow Wayne "Woody" Hayes, but that's where I draw the line.

FOREWORD

LACING UP MY cleats, I hear the familiar booming voice that guided us to this defining moment in Michigan Football History. In his military-esque tone, Bo Schembechler said, "Listen up! We're about to show why we are going to be champions! We've worked hard; we've earned the right to be here." By the time Bo finished with, "Let's go!" the piercing sounds of lockers slamming, and over seventy players screaming, "Let's get 'em!" made it tough for the doubters to continue to ignore what was coming, we were about to arrive!

The thunderous sound of that epic day is reflective of the impact this moment had on Michigan Football. The following pages provide the reader with a window into the icon who put his winning stamp on college football. Barry Gallagher's research and statistics brilliantly tell a story that every one of Bo's players knew each time we were in his presence – he was one of the greatest coaches in football history. He injected a tenacious fighting spirit into a program that many Michigan fans felt was in decline after the 50-14 thrashing a year before to arch-rival Ohio State and Bo's mentor Woody Hayes. At our reunions, no one doubts that Bo was the most motivational and unwaveringly focused individual we had ever known. We were a family and during his time, Bo was the father of hundreds of young warriors.

As we crashed out of the locker room, stormed into the Michigan tunnel and ran onto the field to dismantle the Ohio State Buckeyes, known as the "Team of the Century," in what was called by many broadcasters the "Upset of the Century," we finally arrived and could hear Bo's everlasting words, "Those who stay will be champions."

Glenn Doughty
#22 RB/WR
1869-1971
Big Ten Champion (1969 and 1971) and Rose Bowl Player (1970 and 1972)

INTRODUCTION

I FIRST MET COACH Glenn Edward "Bo" Schembechler in January 1986 when he agreed to do a favor for a retiring co-worker. My co-worker's name was Glenn Elmo Garlough. Glenn was a long-time employee in the Tri-Service Reserve Officers' Training Corps (ROTC) program at The University of Michigan. He was also a military veteran who just happened to be a football season ticket holder and a huge fan of Michigan and Coach Schembechler. I wanted to do something special for his retirement dinner and I came up with the idea of a signed photograph from the famous Michigan coach. About two weeks before the retirement event, I called Bo's office and explained to his secretary what I wanted to do and why it was important. She told me that Coach Schembechler was in the office for about two hours and would be leaving for a recruiting trip. He could see me for a few minutes if I could get there in the next ten minutes. My sign and my camera were already loaded in the car so I quickly exited the ROTC building and traveled from North Hall to the Michigan Athletic Offices in record time.

I waited for about five minutes while Bo finished a phone call and then was ushered in to his office. Wow – I couldn't believe it, I was about to meet the famous Michigan coach in his own office! Coach Schembechler greeted me with a firm handshake and a big smile. "How are you doing Major?" How's the Army treating you? We talked for a good thirty minutes before we got down to the business of taking the picture and getting my gift ready for my friend Glenn.

During our meeting, I told Coach Schembechler about my first Michigan game which was also his first. September 20, 1969 (Band Day) was a special day in my life and his too! I related my memories of that 42-14 win over Vanderbilt. I told him that Glenn Doughty ran for an eighty-yard touchdown and had nearly 140 yards rushing in his first start at Michigan. Bo complimented me for my accurate memory and we shifted to small talk about the Army, family, and other things.

I told Coach about my friend Glenn and why I wanted to take the picture. Coach said that Glenn sounded like a fine American and a great Michigan fan. I assured him that Glenn was exactly that and I knew the picture would mean a lot to him. When I showed Coach the sign, it said, "From one Glenn "E." to another. Happy Retirement." Bo said, okay, I know your friends middle initial is "E", but what is his middle name? When I said it was "Elmo" he said, "Wow I don't think I've ever heard that one before." Coach Schembechler proceeded to write a greeting that said "Best Wishes and Go Blue! He signed it "Bo Schembechler." It was perfect! I took three or four pictures to make sure I had some good ones and was just finishing up when Bo's secretary came in to tell coach that he would have to be leaving for his recruiting trip.

I thanked Bo for his time and for helping me take care of a really good man and a great Michigan fan. Coach Schembechler wished me good luck and I left. I didn't know if I would ever see Coach Schembechler again, but I was thankful for the time we shared.

One of the highlights of my life was the expression on Glenn Elmo Garlough's face when he unveiled the photograph of Coach Schembechler holding the "Happy Retirement" card. We both got some tears in our eyes – it was easily the gift of the night and he received some very nice gifts. None meant more than the picture and the sign. Coach Schembechler didn't have to do what he did, but I am so grateful that he took the time that day.

I know there are thousands of stories like this about Bo Schembechler. Yes, he was a tough, hard driving coach who did get a little excited on the sidelines during practice or a game. Yes, he would yell at game officials too. But, that intense, crazy man on the sidelines was not the same man I met that day. Bo was simply a decent, humble man who truly cared about college football, his players and the Michigan family and fans.

IT ALL STARTED WHEN BO AGREED TO DO A FAVOR FOR MY FRIEND.

CHAPTER ONE

BO AND THE NATION'S BEST

"**B**O WHO?" THAT was one of the headlines in an area paper on December 28, 1968, the day after Don Canham introduced Glenn Edward "Bo" Schembechler as the fourteenth man to coach the Michigan Football team. The rumor was that Canham was going after the guy at Penn State, a fellow named Paterno, Joe Paterno. It was already late December and Canham wanted to hire a coach before the end of the year. He knew that the next guy had to have time to assemble his staff, hit the recruiting trail and get ready for spring football practice. Canham later admitted that Paterno was the first coach that he offered the job to, but Paterno asked for more time since he was getting his team ready for his first bowl game. Paterno would not be ready to make a decision until after the Orange Bowl was played on January 1st, 1969.

Don Canham didn't want to wait that long so he followed up on this Schembechler guy whose name kept surfacing during the research process. Canham invited Schembechler to Ann Arbor - Bo registered at the hotel under a secretive name - the interview went well and that was it! Unlike today, there was no million-dollar contract haggling and no drawn-out negotiations. Bo took the job for a thousand dollar pay raise and no formal contract, just a "five-year" hand shake from a relieved Don Canham. Bo knew that this was the opportunity of a lifetime and he seized it like a fairy tale hero grasps the magical "brass ring." This simple "deal" would eventually mean that Michigan Football, The University of Michigan, the City of Ann Arbor, the State of Michigan and college football would never, ever, be the same! "Bo Who" would simply become "Bo" and everybody, just about everywhere, would know his name!

Glenn Edward "Bo" Schembechler Takes Charge of Michigan Football

Now anybody who knew Bo Schembechler understood that he had the patience of a rattlesnake when it came to coaching football. Five years to rebuild the Michigan Football program, are you kidding? It was nice that Don Canham was talking five years, but Bo knew that the "string" that he was on was a lot shorter than five years. He knew that he was viewed as an outsider and a buckeye to boot! He was not a "Michigan Man" and the history, the expectations, and the fans would demand more than a five-year re-building program. Bo simply rolled up his sleeves and put together a plan to get things turned around in less than five years – a lot less! He knew that Bump Elliott left him some very good players. He also knew what he had to do to make them better, especially against ohio state. No - this would not take five years, not if he had his way and Bo usually got his way!

Bo hit Ann Arbor like a tornado in the middle of January, and you don't see a lot of January tornados in the State of Michigan. Bo was everywhere, getting his feet on the ground, meeting and greeting people in Ann Arbor – selling himself and his program. But mostly, Bo was meeting his players, his staff, his secretaries, the janitors, everybody! He spent a lot of time setting expectations for how the Michigan Football program would operate – everything from answering the phone, to cleaning the uniforms, storing equipment, you name it!

There was a new "sheriff" in town and Bo let everybody know what Sheriff Schembechler expected. It was pretty simple - he just wanted every coach, every player, every equipment manager, every secretary – everybody associated with the Michigan Football Program, to give their best every day. Got it?

Mostly though, he spent a lot of time getting to know his players and getting these poor young men ready for the toughest football season of their lives. They had no idea who they were dealing with - not a clue! They had heard he was a disciplinarian and they heard he was tough. But, an Army Drill Sergeant with a whistle and a yardstick? Wow, where did this crazy guy come from?

Well, like every man, Bo came from a "lot of places." First and foremost, he came from Barberton, Ohio and from his hard-working, honest parents. His sister gave him the nickname "Bo" because she couldn't say "brother" when she was little. Although his father died early, Glenn Edward Schembechler, had a huge impact on Bo and his values and character were set for life.

Bo didn't quibble about right and wrong, hard work, honesty or integrity – those items would never be compromised by him, his coaches or his players – period!

Bo also came from a long line of successful coaches, so he had a complete understanding of what it took to build a successful college football program. He knew about the great history of the University of Michigan Football program, the winged helmets, Yost, Crisler and all that stuff. Also, he spent time in columbus, working for a guy named Hayes, was doing a pretty good job at ohio state. That team in ohio might be something to emulate, minus the scarlet and gray uniforms of course. Finally, Bo spent a little time in the United States Army so, he probably had a little more "bark" than most coaches. So that's a little bit about who he was when he showed up in Ann Arbor. Again, nobody in town was ready for this guy, especially his players!

Spring Football – Also Known as Wolverine Basic Training 1969

Glenn Doughty, a Sophomore on the 1969 team, survived Bo's first Spring Practice program, became a starter and went on to a solid career in the National Football League. He once told me that Marine Basic Training could not have been worse than Bo's conditioning and practice program for Michigan's "ninetieth" football team. It was horribly tough for the players, unlike anything they had ever experienced in their young lives. Bo's take on the team that he had inherited was that they were talented, but not very tough. Schembechler was hell bent to change that assessment - for sure! Bo also had a very good idea what the old man in columbus was doing with his team so Bo never let up. He knew that Woody was pushing his team to be even better than they were in 1968 and they were pretty good that year! Bo also knew that Michigan had been embarrassed by the buckeyes in 1968 and that would never happen again. So, in reality, Bo was establishing a mind-set, an attitude, a toughness that his Wolverines would need to compete with ohio state and everybody else they would play in 1969.

Although the facts differ, it is estimated that about one hundred and fifty young men showed up for Bo's first spring practice session. When "Spring Ball" ended, only about seventy-five to eighty remained. Bo was not upset by this development because he was not looking for quantity, he was looking for quality. The ones who stuck with it were the ones Bo wanted. They were the players he needed to rebuild the Michigan Football program. There were constant protests about the Vietnam War on the Ann Arbor campus during Bo's first few months on campus, but there were no visible protests at Yost Field House where the Wolverines practiced. The new players, the "walk-ons," the returning "stars" and everybody else might have complained, but not to Bo. The ones who couldn't take it simply quit, they went back to the locker room after another brutal practice and never returned. Again, no protests, no signs, and no chants. Again, the players who couldn't cut it just vanished. Those who didn't want to pay the price that Bo and his staff were asking simply walked off and disappeared in dorms and classrooms never to be seen on the football field again.

Those Who Stay Will Be Champions

Bo and his staff knew that they had to separate the "men" from the "boys" if they were going to compete with the buckeyes and the rest of the teams on their schedule. They knew they were asking a lot of any player who wanted to be Schembechler's version of a Michigan Wolverine. Bo and his staff sensed that they needed to come up with a slogan or something that communicated a message that it was all going to be worth it. Six simple words created a vision that a large number of players bought into that first, hellacious spring. *"Those Who Stay Will Be Champions!"* This phrase would become the mantra of Michigan Football for the next twenty-one years and beyond. This statement provided a bold promise of what was to come for the survivors, the believers, the ones who were willing to stick it out. This famous phrase came from a football coach and his staff, not some marketing department at a Fortune 500 company. It wasn't as famous as the Nike phrase, "Just Do It," but it sure worked for Bo and his Michigan Men. Man did it work!

When you take a closer look at the phrase, "Those Who Stay Will Be Champions" you are struck by the absolute certainty of the "promise" that is implied in those six words. What is even more striking is that Coach Schembechler had not won a single Big Ten game as a Michigan head coach, let alone a conference championship. Talk about "Bo-dacious," who was this guy? And, oh by the way, Michigan had only won one conference title (1964) in the last eighteen years. Yet, there was this sign hanging up in the locker room that guaranteed the players who stuck it out would be a Big Ten Champion, maybe a Rose Bowl Champion, or possibly a National Champion before they left the Michigan Football program. Yes, that was a young coach setting the bar very, very high for himself, his coaches and his players!

It was probably easier for the Freshman or Sophomores to believe and maybe even the Juniors. But, how about those Seniors, with only one year of eligibility left? What were they thinking and what would happen to Bo, his sign, his credibility, and his program, if they didn't win at least a share of the Big Ten Title in 1969? This was pretty bold stuff when you think about it, but oh how it all worked out in the end.

Bo was a man on a mission that was crystal clear. His intent was to compress Canham's Five Year Plan into a season-long victory march that would end with a victory over ohio state on November 22, 1969 at Michigan Stadium. Bo was relentless. He pushed everyone in the Michigan Football program harder than they had probably been pushed before. His focus, his intensity, his work ethic was driven into minds, hearts and bodies of every player who donned the Maize and Blue uniform during that critical first year.

Three Hundred and Thirty-Two Days Later

Bo's 1969 Wolverines actually had fewer wins than Bump Elliott's team had the previous year heading into the ohio state game. Elliott's team lost their first game to California and then reeled off eight straight victories before the bottom fell out at columbus. Bo's team had seven wins and two losses (Missouri and Michigan State) before "The Game" so it was hard to argue that the Wolverines had improved that much under their new coach. The "experts" didn't give Bo and his seventeen-point underdogs a chance. The really "smart" football people even doubted if the Minnesota Viking professionals could beat the buckeyes. Still, Bo knew something that nobody else knew. He knew the high price his team paid to be in position to gain revenge against the buckeyes for the 50-14 defeat in 1968. In the end, the 1969 Wolverines won eight games, just like the 1968 team. However, one of those victories was against ohio state (arguably the greatest upset in college football history?) and resulted in a share of the Big Ten championship. Bo had delivered on his promise to his seniors and the rest of the team. For the record, he also kept that promise to every other Wolverine who played his full eligibility from 1969-1989 – "Those Who Stayed Were Champions" – all of them!

Bo's "underdogs" accomplished some great things in his first season, the ninetieth season in Michigan Football History and the 100th season of college football – not a bad start for the coach who was Don Canham's second choice. The impatient buckeye had accomplished what many experts thought was impossible. Michigan stopped the buckeye twenty-two game winning streak, knocked them out of the number one spot in the national rankings, and avenged the debacle from 1968.

Remarkably, it all happened in just 332 days, counting from the day he was hired until the day the Michigan Stadium scoreboard read: Michigan 24 - osu 12. That's how it all started in Ann Arbor for Bo and his Wolverines. But, one game, one season, does not make a career. Let's take a closer look at Bo's entire "body of work" from 1969 to 1989. Maybe we can learn how he put Michigan Football back on the national college football radar.

Overall Team Wins from 1969 to 1989

Here is a summary of my research into the teams that stood out in the years that Bo roamed the Michigan sidelines. Most teams played ten to eleven games during this era and the totals include all bowl wins. (Note-This data was gathered from the College Football Data Warehouse and the USA Today College Football Encyclopedia).

Place	Wins	School
1.	210	Nebraska
2.	199	Oklahoma
3.	196	Penn State
4.	**194**	**Michigan**
5.	194	Alabama
6.	181	ohio state
7.	179	Brigham Young
8.	178	USC
9.	175	Notre Dame
10.	173	Arkansas

His impact was significant to say the least. The Wolverines played fifty-two more games during the Bo Era than in the Ooosterbaan/Elliott Era. Bo won eighty more games (194 compared to 114) in that twenty-one-year period compared to the previous twenty-one years. This worked out to almost four (3.81) more victories per year during the Bo Era. Nationally, this tied them for fourth best along with Alabama. I listed Michigan ahead of Alabama because they won their one hundred and ninety-four games in two hundred and forty-seven chances while the Crimson Tide did it in two hundred forty-eight attempts.

As a historical note, Michigan, ohio state and Arkansas were the only teams in this elite group not to win at least one major national championship during this era. Of course, Bo and Woody were too busy beating each other during this era so each coach ruined the other guy's chances for a national championship starting in 1969 when Bo did the honors to Woody. Bo always said that he would like to win "one of those suckers," but it was never one of the team goals. The focus would always be: Beat osu, win the Big Ten Title and win the Rose Bowl.

You have to give Don Canham credit. The guy he wanted, Joe Paterno, won two more games during this era, so Bo proved to be the next best choice. The Wolverines were no longer "irrelevant" and they were definitely back in the conversations about the country's best football teams. Again, it didn't take five years, it took exactly 332 days, from the late December 1968 press conference to late November 1969 post game celebration. Oh, what a difference a great leader can make!

Coach Schembechler Era – Year One - 1969

Coach "Bo Who" Schembechler converted a lot of Wolverine players and fans into believers after his amazing win over the buckeyes. However, he was smart enough to know that there was a lot more work to be done. As soon as he recovered from his New Year's Eve heart attack in California, he went back to work. He was determined to re-build the Michigan Football program and he wanted to prove that he was the right man for the job of Head Football Coach at The University of Michigan.

A Closer Look at Bo's Key Statistics 1969

Year	Games	Won-Lost-Tied	Scored/Avg.	Allowed/Avg.	+/-
1969	11	8-3-0	352/32.0	148/13.4	+18.6

Season one under Bo Schembechler was better than 1968 mainly because of the huge season ending win over the buckeyes. Statistically, both regular seasons were similar as both teams won eight games and lost two. Bo's first team averaged thirty-two points per game, the highest average since the National Championship team of 1948 that averaged twenty-eight points per game. On defense, Schembechler's Wolverines made improvements from the 1968 team. Coach Elliott's last team gave up just over fifteen (15.5) points per game while Bo's defense only gave up about thirteen (13.4) points per game.

Again, the combination of the two statistics reveals the most defining number of all - the point differential. The 1969 team's positive point differential of just under nineteen (+18.6) points per game was the highest since the twenty-three (+23.2) point difference posted by Bennie Oosterbaan's 1948 powerhouse. This was an improvement of over six points (6.4) per game over Bump Elliott's differential of over twelve (12.2) points per game average in 1968.

Bo implemented a smash mouth offense and a pounding defense that made a big impression on Michigan's opponents in the 1969 season. It was the beginning of something special that was about to unfold over the next twenty seasons. The Michigan Wolverines were no longer "irrelevant" and they were definitely back in the conversations about the country's best football teams. The best was yet to come!

Coach Schembechler Era – The 1970s

The biggest question surrounding Michigan Football in January 1970 was not about the team, it was about Bo. People were concerned about Coach Schembechler's health after he suffered a heart attack on the eve of his first Rose Bowl. By April 1970 Bo let everybody know that he was ready to go!

A Closer Look at Bo's Key Statistics 1970-1979

Year	Games	Won-Lost-Tied	Scored/Avg.	Allowed/Avg.	+/-
1970	10	9-1-0	288/28.8	90/9.0	+19.8
1971	12	11-1-0	421/35.1	83/6.9	+28.2
1972	11	10-1-0	264/24.0	57/5.2	+18.8
1973	11	10-0-1	330/30.	68/6.2	+23.8
1974	11	10-1-0	324/29.5	75/6.8	+22.7
1975	12	8-2-2	324/27.0	130/10.8	+16.2
1976	12	10-2-0	432/36.0	95/7.9	+28.1
1977	12	10-2-0	353/29.4	124/10.3	+19.1
1978	12	10-2-0	372/31.0	105.8.8	+22.2
1979	12	8-4-0	312/26.0	151/12.6	+13.4
Totals	**115**	**96-16-3**	**3420/29.7**	**978/8.5**	**+21.2**

As usual, Bo was right on both counts. Statistically, Version Two of Bo's Wolverines was a better team than Bo's first group. They posted one more win, had two fewer losses, averaged slightly less points on offense, but improved on defense and ended up with a positive point differential of just under twenty points (+19.8) per game, a slight improvement (+1.2) over the point-differential in 1969 They were one step from perfection, but a season ending loss to the buckeyes ruined what would have been an undefeated season and possibly some votes for a National Championship.

Bo's teams kept improving for the next few years and ten-win seasons became the norm as well as some crushing losses to the buckeyes. His teams were characterized by physical toughness on both sides of the ball. Bo's record during the 1970s was the best in college football – nobody did the seventies better than Bo and his Wolverines. The numbers that his teams put on the board were simply staggering. Four of his teams averaged over thirty points per game. Seven of his teams in this era allowed single digit points against averages. Five of his teams averaged a positive point differential of over twenty points per game and two of those averages were over twenty points for a season. In 1971, the one-point loss to Stanford and the infamous tie (10-10) with the buckeyes in 1973 ruined legitimate chances at perfection and possible National Championships.

Overall, Bo's 1970 teams averaged just under thirty points (29.7) per game, allowed slightly more than eight (8.5) points per game and finished with a positive point differential of over twenty-one (21.2) points per game for the decade – incredible! The powerhouse team of 1976 averaged thirty-six points per game and gave up less than eight points per contest. The point differential of over twenty-eight (+28.1) points per game was the best in modern Michigan Football history. When you score a lot of points and don't allow very many, you're going to average almost ten victories (9.6) per season and win about eighty-five percent of your games - any questions?

Coach Schembechler Era – The 1980s

The achievements from year one through the 1970s were so impressive that even Bo had trouble duplicating what he had accomplished in his first eleven seasons. Bo's Wolverines were very good in the 1980's, but they were not as dominant as the first eleven years of his tenure. There are two things that are hard to do. One is to chase our own shadow and the other is to measure up to your own high standards. Coach Schembechler tried to do both in the 1980s, but fell just a little short.

A Closer Look at Bo's Key Statistics 1980-1989

Year	Games	Won-Lost-Tied	Scored/Avg.	Allowed/Avg.	+/-
1980	12	10-2-0	322/26.8	129/10.8	+16.0
1981	12	9-3-0	355/29.6	162/13.5	+13.3
1982	12	8-4-0	345/28.8	204/17.0	+11.8
1983	12	9-3-0	355/29.6	160/13.3	+16.3
1984	12	6-6-0	214/17.8	200/16.7	+1.1
1985	12	10-1-1	342/28.5	98/8.2	+20.3
1986	13	11-2-0	379/29.2	203/15.6	+13.6
1987	12	8-4-0	331/27.6	172/14.3	+13.3
1988	12	9-2-1	361/30.1	167/13.9	+16.2
1989	12	10-2-0	335/27.9	184/15.3	+12.6
Totals	**121**	**90-29-2**	**3339/27.6**	**1679/13.9**	**+13.7**

Bo's teams slipped a little in the 1980s, but still managed to win ninety games along the way. He had one eleven-win season in 1986 which matched the achievement of his 1971 team. However, the number of ten-win seasons declined from six to "only" two. He had three seasons of eight wins and three more nine-win campaigns. The biggest shocker was the six-win struggle in 1984 when very few things went right for Bo and his Wolverines. Michigan continued to be strong on offense, but only one team (1988) averaged thirty points a game compared to four teams in the 1970s.

The biggest decline was on the defensive side where the Wolverines only had one season (1985) where they allowed less than ten points per game compared to six in the 1970s. Only one team in the 1970s allowed an average of over twelve points per game, but eight teams gave up more than twelve- points per game in the 1980s. This, of course, affected the point differentials which were still very good, just not as dominating. Bo had five teams in the 1970s that had point differentials of over twenty points, but only had one (1985) in the 1980s. The worst point differential of the Bo Era was in 1984 when his teams were only about one point (1.1 to be exact) better than their opponents. Bo's teams were strong in the 1980s, but not as dominant. Instead of posting large numbers of twenty-point blowouts, he was now winning more games by "just" a couple of touchdowns and losing a few more here and there.

The Wolverine scoring average slipped from just under thirty (29.7) points per game in the 1970's to just under twenty-eight (27.6) points per game in the 1980s. The number of points allowed per game went up from just over eight (8.5) in the 1970s to about fourteen (13.9) in the 1980s. The point differential remained very positive. However, declined from over twenty-one (+21.2) points per game to just under fourteen (+13.7) which was more than a touchdown per game. The bottom line was still very good, just not as good as the 1970s. Bo's teams averaged nine wins per season in the 1980s, down from just under ten (9.6) in the 1970s and the winning percentage decreased from eighty-five percent to "only" seventy-five percent in the 1980s.

The Schembechler Era – A Final Look at the Key Statistics

Year/s	Games	Won-Lost-Tied	Scored/Avg.	Allowed/Avg.	+/-
1969	11	8-3-0	352/32.0	148/13.4	+18.6
1970s	115	96-16-3	3420/29.7	978/8.5	+21.2
1980s	121	90-29-2	3339/27.6	1679/13.9	+13.7
Total	**247**	**194-48-5**	**7111/28.8**	**2805/11.4**	**+17.4**

When you look at what happened to Michigan Football after Bo's arrival you have to be impressed. He won eighty more games in twenty-one years (114 to 194) which was a significant improvement from the previous era. The average wins per season jumped from just over five (5.43) to slightly more than nine (9.24) and the winning percentage rocketed from sixty percent to almost eighty percent. His teams were absolutely dominant during the 1970s and settled into an excellent level of performance in the 1980s. His positive point differential of over seventeen (+17.4) points per game was an amazing upgrade from an average of about five (+4.8) points per game in the Pre-Bo Era.

Overall, Coach Bo Schembechler had twenty winning seasons in his tenure at Michigan and the one season where he finished even at six wins and six losses. Bo put together an impressive body of work during the twenty-one years he roamed the sidelines at Michigan Stadium. He did just about everything right, but he wasn't perfect so that, in the end, is what his critics focused on. Bo's detractors like to argue that he won a ton of games, yet didn't win enough bowl games. They point out that he won thirteen Big Ten Championships, but should have won a few more. And oh, yes, he came ever so close to perfection on numerous occasions. Unfortunately, Coach Schembechler could never put together a magical season that ended with the last victory of the year and that elusive national championship. Yes, these "shortfalls" may be true, but the man could flat out coach and he did everything with integrity, honesty and class.

Number One and Top Ten Confrontations

The Michigan football schedule provided lots of opportunities to compete with the nation's best teams through a challenging non-conference schedule and the annual run through the Big

Ten gauntlet. Bo's teams didn't fare too well against number one ranked teams. His record was three wins, five losses and one tie in nine games for a winning rate of only thirty-nine percent. However, this was better than the previous twenty-one years since Michigan lost all three games versus a top ranked opponent from 1948 to 1968. Bo coached in a total of thirty-six games against top ten teams during his tenure – his overall record was fifteen wins, twenty losses and one tie. His winning rate of forty-three percent was a slight improvement (+3.5 percent) over the record from 1948 to 1968. Once again, Bo's teams improved on the numbers from the previous era.

Regular Season Non-Conference Matchups

Michigan played twenty-six different opponents in a total of sixty regular season non-conference games during the Bo Era. Most of these games were early season matchups and only one of these matchups was a Homecoming Game (Florida State in 1986). Bo's teams absolutely excelled in these non-conference games from 1969 to 1989 winning seventy-eight percent of these out of league contests.

Don Canham set his coach up for success by scheduling forty-eight of those sixty games at home. Bo took advantage of his Michigan Stadium games and posted a record of thirty-eight victories, eight defeats and two ties (38-8-2) for a winning rate of eighty-one percent in "Bo's House."

Bo won eight of the twelve non-conference road games scheduled during this era for a winning rate of sixty-seven percent. Overall, Bo's Wolverines finished with a non-conference record of forty-six wins, twelve losses and two ties which worked out to a victory rate of over seventy-eight percent (.783).

The table that follows on the next page lists all twenty-six non-conference teams that Bo faced during his tenure at Michigan. It is interesting to note that he played eight different Pacific Ten Conference teams during his era. All of the games were played in either September or October. His overall record was fifteen wins, three losses and one tie (15-3-1) in those games. Why it was so hard to beat those teams in January is something that Bo was never was able to figure out.

Team	Games(s)	Won	Lost	Tied
Arizona	2	2	0	0
Baylor	1	1	0	0
California	2	2	0	0
Colorado	1	1	0	0
Duke	2	2	0	0
Florida State	1	1	0	0
Hawaii	1	1	0	0
Kansas	1	1	0	0
Long Beach State	1	1	0	0
Maryland	2	2	0	0
Miami	2	1	1	0
Missouri	2	1	1	0
Navy	7	7	0	0
Notre Dame	10	4	6	0
Oregon	1	1	0	0
Oregon State	1	1	0	0
Stanford	4	3	0	1
South Carolina	2	1	1	0
Texas A & M	2	2	0	0
Tulane	1	1	0	0
UCLA	4	3	1	0
Vanderbilt	1	1	0	0
Virginia	1	1	0	0
Wake Forest	2	2	0	0
Washington	4	2	2	0
Washington State	2	2	0	0
Total	**60**	**46**	**12**	**2**

Another interesting fact to note about Bo was that he won his first two non-conference games before losing (40-17) to a ninth ranked Missouri team coached by Dan Devine. After that loss, he would not lose another regular season non-conference game for ten years!

Bo's teams had some streaks that were reminiscent of the winning ways that Fielding Yost recorded in the early 1900s. Schembechler's Wolverine teams won seventeen consecutive games and were undefeated for twenty-nine straight non-conference games. From 1970 through 1978, he won fourteen consecutive home games and was undefeated in twenty-five non-conference games in Michigan Stadium.

One more tidbit, Bo's teams didn't play a lot of non-conference road games in the early years and he won his first five. That meant that he did not lose his first regular season non-conference road game until his eleventh season (1980) at Michigan when an eighth rated Notre Dame team beat Bo's fourteenth rated Wolverines (29-27) on a last second field goal. Remember Michigan played a total of fifty-four non-conference games from 1948 to 1968 winning thirty-seven times and losing seventeen games (37-17-0) for a winning rate of just over sixty-eight percent (.685). When all the numbers were in the books, Bo's teams won just over seventy-eight percent (.783) of their non-conference games which was almost a fourteen percent improvement over the previous twenty-one years. Yes, performance in regular season non-conference games improved significantly under Bo's leadership. Any questions?

National Rankings

Bo's mission was to put Michigan Football back on the national radar and the Associated Press (AP) and United Press International (UPI) pollsters took notice starting in 1969. Bo's Wolverines finished in at least one of the national rankings every year except for the injury plagued season of 1984. Michigan had six top five finishes in the AP polls to go along with ten other top ten finishes for a total of sixteen top ten AP rankings. They also finished three more seasons among the top twenty AP teams. The Wolverines finished strong in the UPI polls as well, posting seven top five rankings to go along with nine other top ten finishes for a total of sixteen top ten UPI rankings. They also finished three more seasons among UPI's top twenty teams.

The Wolverines were not ranked by AP in 1982 (8 wins and 4 losses) or 1984. They missed the UPI rankings in 1984 (6-6) and 1987 (8-4). Bo's highest ranked team was his 1985 team that beat Nebraska in the 1986 Fiesta Bowl and finished second in both the AP and UPI polls.

Although he never won a national championship, Bo built a consistent winner at Michigan and definitely put the Wolverines back in the national spotlight.

Bowl Games

Again, Michigan only played in two bowl games from 1948 to 1968 because they weren't that good most of the time and the Big Ten had a rule that only permitted the conference champion to play in the Rose Bowl. The Big Ten also had a no repeat rule so there weren't that many opportunities to go bowling in the Pre-Bo Era.

I could write an entire chapter on Bo and the bowls, but it would not be very much fun and who would read it? Bowl games were absolutely the "Achilles heel" of Coach Schembechler's career at Michigan. His annual mid-Winter hikes to Pasadena and later, to other bowl venues, were full of all kinds of personal drama, on the field controversy, and gut-wrenching disappointments. Bo never made any excuses, but the man could not get a break when it came to bowl games. He had a heart attack for his first one and his shell-shocked Wolverines lost a close one to John McKay and his USC Trojans. He also "won" a game while he was recuperating from heart surgery so he broke even on the bowl games he wasn't healthy enough to coach in. Then, there were the two Rose Bowl classics - the "phantom touchdown" by USC Trojan Charles White and the "phantom holding call" in Bo's last game that kind of topped it all off for his bowl resume. Sometimes, they just played a really good team, or a Heisman Trophy winner, an especially mobile quarterback, there was always something happening in Bo's bowl games, but it usually wasn't good for him or his Wolverines!

There was no doubt about it – bowl games did not bring out the best in Bo's football teams. The joke around Ann Arbor when I lived there (1985 to 1989) was that his wife, Millie, would not serve his cereal in a bowl because she was afraid he would lose it (I know that's cold, but that was the joke). Speaking of bowls, Bo did do the Big Ten a great service when he absolutely went crazy after his 1973 team had played the number one buckeyes to a tie (10-10) and were denied the opportunity to represent the Big Ten by a special vote of the conference athletic directors. Bo was crushed and the story goes that he never spoke to any of the men who voted against his Wolverines again. He did everything to make them feel guilty about the injustice that was done to his team that finished with ten wins, no losses and one tie and didn't go to a bowl game. Bo's public remarks plus the fact that the Big Ten was losing money by not allowing other teams to go to multiple bowl games eventually fixed the bowl problem. Bo always said it was a high price to pay and he was right. Thankfully, the conference finally got it fixed.

Ironically, Bo's 1975 team was the first Big Ten team to go to a bowl game other than the Rose Bowl. Bo's reward was a matchup against third ranked Oklahoma in the 1976 Orange Bowl. The fifth ranked Wolverines played the number three Sooners tough all the way, but lost by eight points (14-6) to the eventual national champions. Bo's teams would play in fifteen straight bowl games starting with Team Ninety-six. For the record, Bo finished with a record of five wins and twelve losses in the seventeen bowl games that his Wolverines played in. However, after losing the first seven bowl games, his teams won five of the last ten, but never more than two in a row. The bowl game results actually reversed in the Bo Era. Whereas, the Pre-Bo era was "low quantity," but "very high quality (2 wins and 0 losses) the Bo Era was "high quantity," but low quality (5 wins and 12 losses). Bo often said that God must have been trying to keep him humble with his bowl record, and it worked! For the record, here is an alphabetical listing of every bowl game that Bo coached during his Michigan career.

Bowl Game	Season	Date	Opponent	Result
Bluebonnet	1981	12/01/1981	UCLA	Won 33-14
Fiesta	1985	01/01/1986	Nebraska	Won 27-23
Gator	1979	12/28/1979	North Carolina	Lost 15-17
Hall of Fame	1987	01/02/1988	Alabama	Won 28-24
Holiday	1984	12/21/1984	Brigham Young	Lost 17-24
Orange	1975	01/01/1976	Oklahoma	Lost 6-14
Rose	1969	01/01/1970	USC	Lost 3-10
Rose	1971	01/01/1972	Stanford	Lost 12-13
Rose	1976	01/01/1977	USC	Lost 6-14
Rose	1977	01/02/1978	Washington	Lost 20-27
Rose	1978	01/01/1979	USC	Lost 10-17
Rose	1980	01/01/1981	Washington	Won 23-6
Rose	1982	01/01/1983	UCLA	Lost 14-24
Rose	1986	01/01/1987	Arizona State	Lost 15-22
Rose	1988	01/01/1989	USC	Won 22-14
Rose	1989	01/01/1990	USC	Lost 10-17
Sugar	1983	01/02/1984	Auburn	Lost 7-9

A Closer Look at the "Margins"

It was very interesting to look at the margins for Bo's two hundred forty-seven games at Michigan. These numbers tell us exactly what we knew about Bo and his time coaching the Wolverines. He coached in some close games that were decided by five points or less. Yes, there were some great wins and some painful losses in the "really" close games. I had no idea that he won twenty-three and lost twenty-three of the really close games, until I crunched the numbers, but that's what the numbers tell us.

In the regular season, he won twenty-one of the really close ones and lost twenty. Bo had less success in the bowl games with a record of two wins and three losses in games decided by five points or less. In games decided by ten points or less, Bo's record was forty-six wins and forty losses, so he won just over fifty-three percent (.535) of the close ones which were about thirty-four percent of all the games he coached at Michigan.

What was really interesting was the fact that not that many games were very close (over sixty-five percent to be exact). Bo coached in a total of one hundred-sixty-two games that were decided by eleven points or more and he won ninety-percent of them. His record in those games was a stellar achievement of one hundred forty-six wins and only sixteen losses. When playing Bo, you needed to keep it close and if you couldn't stay within ten points your chances of winning diminished greatly.

Win Margin & Number of Wins	Loss Margin & Number of Losses
1 to 5 points = 23 wins (2 bowls)	1 to 5 points = 23 losses (3 bowls)
6 to 10 points = 23 wins (1 bowl)	6 to 10 points = 17 losses (9 bowls)
11 to 15 points = 28 wins	11 to 15 points = 4 losses
16 to 20 points = 15 wins (2 bowls)	16 to 20 points = 2 losses)
21 to 25 points = 21 wins	21 to 25 points = 1 loss
26 or more points = 82 wins	26 or more points = 9 losses

The "margins" clearly show that the Wolverines were a force in college football under Bo Schembechler's leadership. They won their share of close ones (games decided by ten points or less) dominated teams in games decided by eleven or more points. Every team that Bo put on the field was prepared and it showed.

The losses were memorable because they weren't that frequent. Blowout losses were unusual – Missouri (40-17)) in 1969 and Iowa (26-0) in 1984 – that's it! The rest of the time the Wolverines were going to get after you and give you all you could handle and win almost eighty percent of the time. In "blowout" games decided by twenty-one to thirty points Bo's Wolverines won forty-one of forty-three games. That's a winning rate of over ninety-five percent (.953). In games decided by thirty-one to sixty-one points Michigan was perfect winning all sixty-two games of this type.

Bo did his job and so did his coaches and players. Michigan Football was back when he left the Rose Bowl on January 1, 1990. I am sure there was some disappointment, especially with the phantom holding call, but Bo had to know it was a job well done and done right!

All-Americans

Again, Michigan had some quality players in the Pre-Bo Era, but not enough of them. A total of thirteen players were named All-Americans seventeen times from 1948 to 1968, but there were nine seasons where they had no players selected for All-American team recognition. The Wolverines did not have a single All-American selection from 1958 to 1963.

Bo said more than once that he didn't really like recruiting, but he was good at and he had a plan for getting some of the best talent in Michigan, Ohio and other places to come and play for the Maize and Blue. Bo had a very organized, thorough, and productive recruiting system that he learned from Ara and Woody and refined over the years. This system, and the talented coaches that he had on his staff, allowed Michigan to produce some outstanding football players during the Bo Era. Bo enhanced the Michigan All-American tradition as more and more of the top talent in the nation arrived to play in Michigan Stadium.

Bo coached forty players who earned a total of forty-six All-American selections during his coaching tenure. One of his players, Anthony Carter, was selected three times (1980, 81, 82). Four other players, Dave Brown (1973 and & 1974), Mark Donahue (1976-77), Jon Elliott (1986 & 1987) and Mark Messner (1987 & 1988) were selected twice for All-American level performance. So, again, Bo was doing something right. He was recruiting some very talented players and the Michigan Coaching Staff brought out the best in these outstanding athletes. The significant improvement in the number of All-American players (13 to 40) was just another indicator that Bo was moving Michigan Football back where it needed to be - among college football's best!

Here is a listing of the Michigan Football players who earned All-American honors from 1969 to 1989 by position with the offensive positions listed in the first grouping and the defensive positions listed second.

Bo's Offensive All-Americans (22)

Center – Walt Downing (1977), George Lilja (1980), Tom Dixon (1983), John Vitale (1988)

End – James M. Mandich (1969)

Halfback – William Taylor (1971), Rob Lytle (1976), Harold "Butch" Woolfolk (1981)

Offensive Guard – Reggie McKenzie (1971), Mark Donahue (1976-77), Kurt Becker (1981), Stefan Humphries (1983)

Offensive Tackle – Dan Dierdorf (1970), Paul Seymour (1972), Bill Dufek (1976), Ed Muransky (1981) William "Bubba" Paris (1981), John Elliott (1986-1987)

Quarterback – Rick Leach (1978), Jim Harbaugh (1986)

Wide Receiver – Jim Smith (1976), Anthony Carter (1980, 1981, 1982)

Bo's Defensive All-Americans (18)

Defensive Back – Thom Darden (1971), Randy Logan (1972), Dave Brown (1973-74), Don Dufek (1975), Brad Cochran (1985), Garland Rivers (1986)

Defensive Tackle – David Gallagher (1973), Curtis Greer (1979), Mike Hammerstein (1985), Mark Messner (1987-88)

Linebacker - Marty Huff (1970), Mike Taylor (1971), Calvin O'Neal (1976) John Anderson (1977), Ron Simpkins (1979)

Middle Guard – Henry Hill (1970)

Safety – Thomas N. Curtis (1969), Tripp Welborne (1989)

Summary

So, Bo did a pretty good job for the second-choice guy, don't you think? He did everything he could to return Michigan Football to the conversation about the best football programs in the country and by every measurable category (ok–except bowl wins and a national championship or two) he raised his program's performance in a significant way. He did it all with an enormous amount of hard work, dedication, enthusiasm and energy. The man might have been a buckeye when he arrived in Ann Arbor, but his blood ran Maize and Blue by the time he left the sidelines. He loved Michigan and revitalized the "Michigan Man" tradition." He always honored the coaches and players who came before him and he ensured that every player who completed their eligibility had a friend for life.

The Michigan Football program was no longer in decline. Wolverine coaches and players had worked extremely hard for twenty-one years to get Michigan back where Michigan felt it belonged – among the best! Don Canham and Bo formed an unstoppable team on the field and in the stands like Charles Baird and Fielding Yost in the early days of Michigan Football. The value of the "Michigan Football Brand" increased significantly from 1969 to 1989 thanks to Don Canham's marketing genius and Bo's winning football teams. The Michigan Athletic Department was making more money than ever and supporting a large number of Wolverine sports programs in the process. Thanks to Bo, and his amazing run, the Michigan Athletic Department's "Bottom Line" was looking good and the Wolverine Football program was positioned for continued greatness.

Bennie/Bump and Bo vs The Nation - Key Statistics Comparison 1948-1989

Category	1948-1968	1969-1989
Total Wins	114	194
Average Wins/Season	5.43	9.24
National Championships	1	0
Total Games Played	195	247
Overall Winning Percentage	.600	.796
Number of Winning Seasons	14	20
Number of Losing Seasons	7	0
Number of Even Seasons	0	1
# of Non-Conference Games	54	60
Non-Conference Wins	37	46
Non-Conference Losses	17	12
Non-Conference Ties	0	2
Non-Conference Winning %	.685	.783
Non-Conference Home Wins	30	38
Non-Conference Home Losses	14	8
Non-Conference Home Ties	0	2
Non-Conference Home Win %	.682	.810
Non-Conference Road Wins	7	8
Non-Conference Road Losses	3	4
Non-Conference Road Win %	.700	.667
Longest Non-Conference Win Streak	7	17
Longest Non-Conference Losing Streak	6	2
Number of Years Top 5 Final Ranking	2	7
Number of Years Top 10 Final Ranking	3	16
Number of Years Top 20 Final Ranking	4	20
Number of Years Not Ranked	12	1
Number of Bowl Victories	2	5
Number of All-American Selections	17	45

BO AND BUMP ELLIOTT AT THE PRESS CONFERENCE ANNOUNCING THE CHANGING OF THE GUARD AT MICHIGAN IN LATE-DECEMBER 1968.

CHAPTER TWO

BO AND THE BIG TEN

DON CANHAM HIRED Bo for a lot of reasons and one of the biggest was his experience in the Big Ten Conference. He worked as a graduate assistant at osu for Woody Hayes before he moved on to assistant coach positions at Presbyterian College and Bowling Green. He worked in one of the Big Ten's worst programs for two years. Bo tried to help a former Miami teammate, Ara Parseghian, turn around the struggling Northwestern program. He felt like he was bailing out on his friend when Woody Hayes called to offer Bo a paid position at osu, but he knew it was a great opportunity to learn more from the man he played for at Miami. With Ara's blessing, Bo went to work for Woodrow W. Hayes and became Woody's most trusted assistant and heir apparent to succeed Woody whenever the "Old Man" decided to call it quits.

Bo knew the Big Ten. He understood the history, the traditions, and, most importantly, the conference style which was still pretty much about "smash mouth" and "three yards and a cloud of dust" football. Bo understood that style of play and implemented it successfully at Miami of Ohio. Don Canham was banking that he could do the same at Michigan so that the Wolverines could compete with osu. Mr. Canham knew that Michigan had some good returning players, but they needed a little more "smash" to be tough enough to compete for the conference championship. Bo had a lot of good characteristics and "smash" just happened to be one of them.

Again, the Big Ten Conference was balanced during the Oosterbaan-Elliott Era. Lots of programs were fielding competitive teams and winning their fair share of conference championships or co-championships. Recently, however, Duffy Daugherty's Spartans and Woody's buckeyes were doing much better in the conference than Michigan so, Bo knew who he had to beat. Bo was confident that he could turn Michigan around, but he had to do it his way so that's what he did.

Here is a closer look at some key indicators that will tell us how Bo's methods worked in the conference. Again, I used a variety of criteria to measure Michigan's success against the rest of the Big Ten Conference during the Bo Era. First, I looked at overall wins against all opponents from 1969 to 1989. Second, I totaled the number of conference wins that Michigan earned in this time period and compared it to the rest of the teams in the Big Ten. Third, I detailed the number of conference home wins that Bo's Wolverines posted during this time period. Fourth, I totaled the number of conference wins that Michigan was able to earn on the road. Fifth, I looked at the number of conference championships the Wolverines were able to win during this time period and how it compared to the other nine conference teams. Sixth, I summarized Bo's record against all conference teams during this period. Seventh, I examined how the wins and losses translated into conference finishes during this twenty-one year period. Finally, I detailed the number of All-Conference players that played at Michigan during these twenty-one years. An in-depth analysis at all these factors yields a clear picture of Bo's impact on the Michigan's Big Ten Conference performance from 1969 to 1989.

Overall Wins from 1969 to 1989

So how well did the Wolverines stack up against the rest of the conference in overall wins during the Bo Era? How about dominating? How about stunning? How about the best record in the conference for overall wins, conference wins and everything else? Bo's Wolverines were very, very good in league play and they set the conference standard during this time period. Let's take a closer look at the legendary numbers Michigan Football achieved in Big Ten play during the tenure of Glenn Edward "Bo" Schembechler.

Here are the overall records posted by all conference teams from 1969 to 1989. These statistics include all bowl games during this era. Most teams played ten to eleven games during this period. However, some teams played more because the conference changed their outdated bowl game policy so more teams went to more bowl games. (Note-This data was gathered from the Bentley Historical Library, the College Football Data Warehouse and the USA Today College Football Encyclopedia).

Big Ten Conference - Overall Team Records 1969 to 1989

Team	Games	Won	Lost	Tied	Win %
Michigan	**247**	**194**	**48**	**5**	**.796**
osu	242	181	56	5	.760
Michigan State	234	118	109	7	.520
Iowa	240	112	122	6	.480
Purdue	232	108	120	4	.470
Illinois	234	101	125	8	.450
Minnesota	232	100	127	5	.440
Wisconsin	233	95	132	6	.420
Indiana	233	88	142	3	.380
Northwestern	230	49	178	3	.220
Totals	**2357**	**1146**	**1159**	**52**	**.497**

The numbers clearly show that Michigan was the best team in the Big Ten during the Bo Era. The numbers also revealed a weaker conference than in the Pre-Bo Era. There were only three conference teams that had winning records in this time period compared to six teams from 1948 to 1968. Clearly, the Big Ten was no longer one of the stronger conferences in college football.

Bo's Conference Record From 1969 to 1989

Again, the numbers below clearly show that Michigan had the best conference record during Bo's tenure. It is also obvious that the conference was dominated by the Wolverines and the buckeyes. Michigan State was the only other conference team to win more than half of their league games during this time period.

The evidence is overwhelming that the conference had become the "Big Two" (Michigan and osu) and the "little eight" (the rest of the Big Ten). The Wolverines and buckeyes were slugging it out for the conference title just about every year for Bo's first ten years while the rest of the league was fighting for third place and below. Bo and Woody simply dominated the rest of the conference while preparing for their annual championship showdown. Yes, they slipped once in a while, and one of them would get upset, but those incidents were rare. The "Ten Year War" put Michigan and osu at the center of everything that was going on in the conference from the first game of the season to the annual showdown in November.

Bo's goal upon arriving in Ann Arbor was to field a team that would compete with osu every year. He focused intently upon that goal and in the process built a powerhouse football program that enabled him to stand his ground against the buckeyes and beat just about everybody else in the league almost every year.

Check out the numbers on the next page to see how Bo's teams measured up in conference games during his coaching tenure. His winning percentage of eighty-five percent is the highest ever recorded by a Big Ten Coach with over fifty wins.

Big Ten Conference Season Team Records 1969 to 1989

Team	Games	Won	Lost	Tied	Win %
Michigan	**170**	**143**	**24**	**3**	**.850**
osu	168	132	34	2	.791
Michigan State	170	91	73	6	.556
Illinois	170	80	83	7	.491
Purdue	170	82	86	2	.488
Iowa	170	79	85	6	.480
Minnesota	172	67	101	4	.401
Wisconsin	172	65	103	4	.389
Indiana	170	56	112	2	.335
Northwestern	176	39	135	2	.227
Totals	**1708**	**834**	**836**	**38**	**.499**

Yes, there were some painful upsets when Purdue, Minnesota, or Iowa would knock them off from their Number One National Ranking, but Bo's domination of the Big Ten Conference conjured up comparisons to Fielding Yost's exploits in the early 1900's. Yes, Bo had a Big Ten pedigree when he walked into Don Canham's office for his interview. Mr. Canham later said that he knew within fifteen minutes that Bo was the right man for the job. Bo proved him right, didn't he?

Coach Schembechler's Conference Record – Home Games

The wins at Michigan Stadium had been declining for most of the 1960's and so was attendance. Don Cahnam was intent on fixing both problems as soon as possible. For the first time in twenty-one years a non-Michigan Man was hired to improve results in the won-loss column and at the ticket window. Would Bo Schembechler be the man to make it all happen? There was a lot riding on the decision to hire Bo Schembechler, you might say that Don Canham bet his career on Bo. It was that big! Let's see how well Bo did at winning Big Ten home games and helping to get more people in the seats at cavernous Michigan Stadium.

A Closer Look at Bo's Big Ten Home Game Statistics 1969

Year*	Games	Won-Lost-Tied	Scored/Avg.	Allowed/Avg	+/- Difference
1969	3	3-0-0	90/30.0	39/13.0	+17.0

*Bold Year = Big Ten Championship Season

Bo's home numbers in year one were very good, but not as good as the numbers that Bump Elliott's squad posted the year before. Bump's 1968 team averaged just under thirty-three points (32.8) per home conference game versus Bo's team that averaged thirty points per contest. On defense, Bump's last team was better too - allowing just under eleven points (10.8) per home game compared to an average of seventeen points per game for Bo's team. Both sets of numbers produced similar results as Bump's team went undefeated at home in conference play in 1968 (4-0-0) and Bo's team won three of three conference games in Michigan Stadium in 1969. I am sure that Bo considered it something to build on and that is all I will say about that for now.

Coach Schembechler – Conference Home Games 1970s

Bo's conference home game resume started off very well, but it got much better, especially for the next six years. Bo won every conference home game for his first six seasons. He did have the infamous tie with osu in 1973, but that was it. Michigan Stadium was Bo's House long before it became the Big House. Bo did not lose his first home conference game until Woody and his buckeyes got him in the last game of his seventh season (1975) at Michigan.

So, after his first seven seasons, Bo's home conference record stood at twenty-five wins, one loss and one tie. When you win over ninety-four percent of your home conference games lots of good things start happening. If you are doing anything on the road, you are in position to compete for the Big Ten title every year and that's exactly what Bo did. If you are winning all those home conference games, the fans will show up and that's also what happened. In fact, the third and last home conference home win in 1975 was the start of Michigan's incredible attendance streak of crowds of one hundred thousand fans or more. A streak that is still going strong today! Check out the numbers that Bo's Wolverine's achieved during the decade of the seventies.

A Closer Look at Bo's Big Ten Home Game Statistics 1970 -1979

Year	Games	Won-Lost-Tied	Scored/Avg.	Allowed/Avg.	+/- Difference
1970	4	4-0-0	170/42.5	33/8.2	+34.3
1971	4	4-0-0	169/42.2	27/6.7	+35.5
1972	4	4-0-0	68/17.0	6/1.5	+15.5
1973	4	3-0-1	115/28.7	35/8.7	+20.0
1974	4	4-0-0	145/36.2	14/3.5	+32.7
1975	4	3-1-0	166/41.5	28/7.0	+34.5
1976	4	4-0-0	165/41.2	44/11.0	+30.2
1977	4	4-0-0	156/39.0	40/10.0	+29.0
1978	4	3-1-0	112/28.0	43/10.0	+18.0
1979	5	4-1-0	176/35.2	67/13.4	+21.8
Totals	41	37-3-1	1442/35.2	326/7.9	+27.2

*Bold Year = Big Ten Championship Season

Bo's teams definitely made the best of the home field advantage in conference play at Michigan Stadium, especially for the first eleven years of his tenure. The numbers Schembechler put up for his conference home games were simply ridiculous! His teams accomplished impressive home feats that had never been seen at Michigan Stadium. The Wolverines had seven undefeated home conference seasons in ten years. In short, they were simply dominant. They scored an average of thirty-five points per game and allowed about seven points per game for the decade of the 1970s. His teams were strong on both sides of the ball. Four teams averaged over forty-points for every home game for four seasons (1970, 1971, 1975 and 1976) and came close to that in 1977 when they scored an average of thirty-nine points per game. Every team but the 1972 team averaged over twenty-eight points per game, a truly impressive feat!

The defensive numbers were equally impressive. The 1972 team only allowed six points in four home victories which averaged out to less than two points (1.5) per game. They only scored an average of seventeen points per game at home that season, but still posted an impressive point differential of almost plus sixteen (+15.5). Bo's defenses allowed single digit points per game averages in seven of the ten years of the decade. The plus and minus point differences were all positive and averaged over thirty points per game for six seasons in the 1970s. Bo managed to post an average point differential of plus twenty-seven points (+27.2) per game in the 1970s which put him ahead of everyone in the conference. It is amazing that he lost three home games with those kinds of numbers, but that is the nature of the Big Ten, especially when rivals like osu and MSU come to town.

The stunning numbers that Bo's teams put on the score board allowed his teams to post an incredible record of thirty-seven wins, only three losses and one infamous tie (37-3-1) in forty-one conference home games during the 1970s.

This worked out to a phenomenal winning rate of just under ninety-two percent (.915). This kind of performance at home put Michigan in position to challenge for the Big Ten title every year. In addition, such a record also boosted Mr. Canham's bottom line which made him a very happy athletic director. Attendance improved steadily during Bo's first eight years and by 1975, Michigan's attendance was hitting record marks and would continue to do so for the rest of Bo's tenure and beyond!

Coach Schembechler – Conference Home Games 1980s

Coach Schembechler's conference home game numbers in the 1970s were staggering so it would be hard for anyone to duplicate this level of performance for another decade. Of course, that's exactly what Bo set out to do and he came close, very close. Bo really set the bar high for his teams heading into the 1980s. Let's see how well his Michigan Men measured up to the standards that his teams had established in the previous eleven years.

Bo's teams continued to perform superbly in their home conference games in the 1980s. Although the numbers declined slightly in all areas, the differences were minimal. Coach Schembechler's Wolverines posted six undefeated home conference seasons including two seasons of five wins each (1982 and 1983). He had nine winning seasons in ten years, but did endure his first, and only, two loss home-season in 1981 when the Wolverines broke even at home in four conference games.

For the true number-crunchers out there the winning rate between the two decades declined from just under ninety-two percent (.915) in the 1970s to just over eighty-eight percent (.883) – a difference of just over three percent (-3.2) percent. That's about as consistent as you can get for two decades of football.

A Closer Look at Bo's Big Ten Home Game Statistics 1980-1989

Year*	Games	Won-Lost-Tied	Scored/Avg.	Allowed/Avg.	+/- Difference
1980	4	4-0-0	115/28.7	47/11.7	+17.0
1981	4	2-2-0	124/31.0	44/11.0	+21.0
1982	5	5-0-0	179/35.8	71/14.2	+21.6
1983	5	5-0-0	160/32.0	62/12.4	+19.6
1984	5	4-1-0	115/23.0	58/11.6	+11.4
1985	4	4-0-0	149/37.2	38/9.5	+27.7
1986	4	3-1-0	133/33.2	56/14.0	+19.2
1987	4	3-1-0	135/33.7	39/9.7	+23.5
1988	4	4-0-0	108/27.0	25/6.2	+20.8
1989	4	4-0-0	132/33.0	55/13.7	+19.3
Totals	43	38-5-0	1350/31.3	495/11.5	+19.8

*Bold Year = Big Ten Championship Season

Again, Coach Schembechler's Wolverines were strong on both sides of the ball in Bo's House during the 1980s. His teams continued to score big and defend tenaciously, making it difficult for visiting Big Ten opponents to win at Michigan Stadium. Michigan averaged over thirty points per game for seven years and scored an average of just over thirty-one points per game during the 1980s. Again, this was a slight decline of about four points per game (3.9) from the seventies. All of Bo's teams scored an average of at least twenty-three points per game during the eighties.

The defensive numbers declined the most, but continued to be very good. Only three teams held opponents to an average of less than ten points per game (9.5 in 1985, and 9.7 in 1987) with the 1988 team's average of just over six points (6.2) per game being the best of the decade. The Wolverines allowed an average of just over eleven points (11.5) per game for the decade of the 1980s – an increase of about three points (3.6) per game. These numbers, combined with the slight decrease in Wolverine scoring, still gave Michigan plenty of room in the point differentials. The plus and minus point differences were all positive for the decade and five were over twenty points per game.

Overall, Michigan had a very strong performance in conference home games in the decade of the 1980s. Again, the combination of high scoring (31.3 points per game) and stingy defense (11.5 points allowed per game) yielded a positive point differential of just under twenty points per game (19.8) for the decade. That number is a strong indicator that Michigan won a lot of games in this decade. In fact, they posted one more win in the eighties that they did in the seventies, but they also had two more losses and did not have any ties. The final numbers for the 1980s looked like this: thirty-eight wins, five losses and no ties (38-5-0) for a winning rate of just over eighty-three percent (.833).

Coach Schembechler - Conference Home Game Summary and Statistics 1969-1989

Is there any doubt that Bo Schembechler was the greatest coach in Michigan Stadium History? His teams won more games in the Big House than anyone ever has or probably ever will! Yes, Bo's House is the right way to describe Michigan Stadium from 1969 to 1989. Bo knew how to keep the home fans happy, just win baby, just win. Coach Schembechler's winning ways in conference play put him in contention for the Big Ten title just about every year. The injury bug got him in 1984 and some bad breaks hurt him in 1987, otherwise the Wolverines were always in the hunt and were very difficult to beat at home. Take a look at the numbers that Bo's Wolverines achieved at Michigan Stadium from 1969 to 1989:

Year(s)	Games	Won-Lost-Tied	Scored/Avg.	Allowed/Avg.	+/- Difference
1969	3	3-0-0	90/30.0	39/13.0	+17.0
1970s	41	37-3-1	1442/35.2	326/7.9	+27.2
1980s	43	38-5-0	1350/31.3	495/11.5	+19.8
Totals	87	78-8-1	2882/33.1	860/9.9	+23.2

When you look at Bo's body of work for Big Ten Conference home games you have to be amazed. His teams scored an average of just over thirty-three points (33.1) per game in eighty-seven games and allowed an average of just under ten points (9.9) per conference game at Bo's House. His positive point differential of over twenty-three points per game (+23.2) helps explain why he won so many games in Michigan Stadium. Bo's overall record in home games finished at seventy-eight victories, eight defeats and one tie (78-8-1) for a lofty winning percentage of just over ninety percent (.902) – wow! I just don't see anyone maintaining this level of performance for as long as Bo did, not going to happen. He was the best, simply the best ever, at The Big House! Any questions?

Coach Schembechler's Conference Record – Road Games

Bo knew that the road to a Big Ten Championship always traveled through some nasty places like East Lansing, Lafayette, Minneapolis and that terrible horseshoe field in columbus. Bo understood that he would have to win a fair share of his road games in order to have a shot at the conference title every season. His Big Ten "road show" got off to a bad start when he took his Wolverines to East Lansing for the first time in October 1969. It was a long ride back to Ann Arbor as Bo and his coaches and players pondered an eleven-point defeat (MSU 23- UM 12). The only thing that is worse than losing your first conference road game is losing it to your in-state rivals. Bo knew that he had some work to do to win on the road and in the State of Michigan.

A Closer Look at Bo's Big Ten Road Game Statistics - 1969

Year*	Games	Won-Lost-Tied	Scored/Avg.	Allowed/Avg	+/- Difference
1969	4	3-1-0	155/38.8	38/9.5	+29.3

*Bold Year = Big Ten Championship Season

Bo and his staff got things figured out in a hurry as they destroyed Minnesota, Illinois and Iowa in the final three road games of his first season. They must have decided that they were going to be rude guests when they ventured into another Big Ten stadium and that's exactly what they started to do. As you can see from the chart, they dominated their final three conference opponents on the road. So the 1969 season was a good start for the rookie coach, but Bo knew that he and his Wolverines had plenty of room for improvement in 1970.

Coach Schembechler – Conference Road Game Statistics - 1970 to 1979

You can see from the numbers on the chart that follows that Bo won his fair share of Big Ten road games, and a bunch of everyone else's share as well. His Wolverines produced four undefeated conference road show seasons in 1971, 1973, 1975 and 1978. You only needed three fingers to count the teams that were able to beat Michigan in their own stadium in the seventies. The buckeyes were the biggest thorn in Bo's side as they won the first three road games of the decade, but did not defeat Bo again in columbus until the eighties. Bo's stellar road record combined with his outstanding home record gave him a chance to compete for the Big Ten title every season.

A Closer Look at Bo's Big Ten Road Game Statistics - 1970 to 1970

Year*	Games	Won-Lost-Tied	Scored/Avg.	Allowed/Avg.	+/- Difference
1970	3	2-1-0	67/22.3	35/11.7	+10.6
1971	4	4-0-0	94/23.5	28/7.0	+14.2
1972	4	3-1-0	94/23.5	28/7.0	+16.5
1973	4	4-0-0	130/32.5	23/5.7	+26.8
1974	4	3-1-0	69/17.3	45/11.3	+6.0
1975	4	4-0-0	88/22.0	48/12.0	+10.0
1976	4	3-1-0	109/27.3	23/5.8	+21.5
1977	4	3-1-0	101/25.3	46/11.5	+13.8
1978	4	4-0-0	149/37.3	17/4.3	+33.0
1979	3	2-1-0	69/23.0	38/12.7	+10.3
Totals	38	32-6-0	976/25.6	346/9.1	+16.5

*Bold Year = Big Ten Championship Season

Bo's road numbers were almost too good to believe. The man went on the road and won as if he was coaching in Bo's House instead of a football field in enemy territory. Coach Schembechler's teams scored big on the road in most conference seasons in the seventies. They had two seasons where they averaged over thirty points per game as the "visitors" and only posted one season (1975) where they failed to score an average of more than twenty-three points per game on somebody else's conference field.

When you combine the offensive output with some very stingy defenses, you begin to see why Bo's teams were so dominant on the road in their conference games of the seventies. The Wolverines had four seasons where they allowed single digit point production and the high for this ten year period was only about twelve points (12.7) per game in 1979. The bottom line was that the conference road game point differentials were positive for every season and were in double digits for every season but 1974. Michigan's outstanding play on both sides of the ball translated into a lot of good things for Bo and his Wolverines.

There is no disputing that Bo was a very rude guest in the seventies. His conquering heroes made shambles of most conference teams in their own stadiums as the Wolverines averaged over twenty-five points (25.6) per game on the road and allowed just over nine points per game (9.1). The positive point differential of over sixteen points per game (+16.5) helped to produce a record of stellar record of thirty-two wins and only six losses (32-6-0) in thirty-eight conference road games. His conference road winning percentage for the decade was a stunning eighty-four percent!

Coach Schembechler – Conference Road Game Statistics - 1980 to 1989

Once again, it was Bo's own fault that people expected so much from him and his Wolverine Football team. His amazing conference road winning rate set the bar really high for his teams. Bo expected his teams to be good at home and on the road and now, after eleven years, the fans came to expect it too. Let's see how well the Michigan footballers did in the eighties version of Bo's Conference "Road Show."

A Closer Look at Bo's Big Ten Road Game Statistics - 1980 to 1989

Year*	Games	Won-Lost-Tied	Scored/Avg.	Allowed/Avg.	+/- Difference
1980	4	4-0-0	105/26.3	17/4.3	+22.0
1981	5	4-1-0	152/30.4	81/11.2	+14.2
1982	4	3-1-0	108/27.0	55/13.8	+13.2
1983	4	3-1-0	144/36.0	47/11.8	+24.2
1984	4	1-3-0	49/12.3	84/21.0	-8.7
1985	4	2-1-1	92/23.0	22/5.5	+17.5
1986	4	4-0-0	129/32.3	62/15.5	+16.8
1987	4	2-2-0	68/17.0	65/16.3	+.70
1988	4	3-0-1	165/41.3	69/17.3	+24.0
1989	4	4-0-0	109/27.3	44/11.0	+16.3
Totals	41	30-9-2	1121/27.3	546/13.3	+14.0

*Bold Year = Big Ten Championship Season

In the decade of the eighties, Bo and his Wolverines were almost human in their exploits. Schembechler lost a total of nine conference road games in this era as five teams beat him once (Illinois, Indiana, Michigan State, Purdue and Wisconsin). Iowa and ohio state were able to defend their home turf two times each against Bo's invaders. Northwestern and Minnesota played gracious hosts in the decade allowing Michigan victories on every visit. Michigan also posted ties in this era against Illinois (1985) and Iowa (1988).

In 1984, after sixteen years on the sidelines, Bo's Wolverines finally lost more than one conference game on the road. Actually, Michigan lost three road games that year without starting quarterback Jim Harbaugh to lead them. They suffered through defeats at Iowa, Purdue, and ohio state and finished with a record of one win and three losses in away games that year. The 1987 team also experienced more than one road loss when they finished with two victories and two defeats in four road trips that season.

Once again, the Wolverines put up some impressive offensive numbers in conference away games during the eighties. Average points scored in this decade's conference road games actually increased by almost two points per game. The Wolverines averaged over forty-one points per Big Ten road game in 1988 and averaged at least thirty points per game in 1981, 1983 and 1986. Scoring was not a problem except for 1984 and in 1987 when they only averaged seventeen points per road contest.

The defense slipped a little in the eighties as the Wolverines allowed their conference hosts to score an average of just over thirteen points (13.3) per game versus about nine points (9.1) per game in the seventies. The best defenses of this decade were in 1980 (average of 4.3 points allowed per game) and 1985 (average of 5.5 points allowed per game). Overall, Bo's defenders were pretty consistent for most of the decade allowing about fifteen points per contest. The 1984 season, again, was the worst of the decade (21.0 points allowed per game) because the offense was not scoring much and they spent a lot of time on the field. When the defensive numbers were combined with the offensive output of this decade – the point differentials were still good enough to produce some very positive outcomes for the Wolverines.

Michigan achieved some very high positive point differentials in the eighties. The Wolverines posted three seasons with positive differentials of twenty-two or more which included a decade high of twenty-four points per game in 1988. Bo's Footballers had five more seasons where they had positive point differentials in the thirteen to seventeen range. The 1987 team posted the lowest positive point differential of Bo's career when they were only about one point (.70) better than their conference hosts. The only negative point differential of Bo's twenty-one year Big Ten road show was "achieved" in 1984 when the Wolverines were about minus nine (-8.7) for the season. This dubious number explained why Bo's team was only able to win one road game out of four in that injury filled season.

Overall, the numbers were still better than most as they finished with a record of thirty wins, nine losses and two ties in (30-9-2) in forty-one conference road games. These numbers produced a winning percentage of about seventy-five percent (.756) which was good enough to help win five more conference titles during the eighties.

Coach Schembechler – Conference Road Game Statistics Summary 1969-1989

Here is a summary of Bo's road game statistics from 1969 to 1989. Amazing!

Year(s)	Games	Won-Lost-Tied	Scored/Avg.	Allowed/Avg.	+/- Difference
1969	4	3-1-0	155/38.8	38/9.5	+29.3
1970s	38	32-6-0	976/25.6	346/9.1	+16.5
1980s	41	30-9-2	1121/27.3	546/13.3	+14.0
Totals	**83**	**65-16-2**	**2252/27.1**	**930/11.2**	**+15.9**

Coach Schembechler's teams were road warriors. They had a plan for every road game and it usually worked out well for Michigan, but not for their conference hosts. Bo's Wolverines allowed him to compete for a Big Ten title in just about every season because of their stellar play in other Big Ten stadiums. Here is a summary of the numbers, the very impressive numbers, that enabled the Wolverines to win a ton of conference road games and titles from 1969 to 1989.

All of the numbers listed above translated into something very special for Bo and his band of Michigan Men over the course of his career. Nobody scores an average of twenty-seven points on the road for twenty-one seasons, are you kidding me? Only allowing the host team to score just over eleven points per game is ridiculous. A positive point differential of almost sixteen points per game meant that Bo and his Wolverines were favored to win by two touchdowns, two extra points and a safety every time they hit the road. The numbers above easily explained why Bo won almost eighty percent (.795) of his road games while he was at Michigan. Nobody was ever that good, not Fielding Yost, not Fritz Crisler, not Bennie Oosterbaan. I'm sorry Wolverine Fans - no Michigan coach will ever come close to these numbers, period.

Coach Schembechler's Final Conference Record – 1969 to 1989

Bo Schembechler proved to be the perfect hire for Don Canham and Michigan. His Big Ten pedigree and his knowledge of osu and Coach Hayes allowed him to compete and win consistently in the Big Ten Conference. Let's take a look at the Bo's Conference Resume from 1969 to 1989. This final look at his Big Ten performance will summarize all conference games, home and road, and paint an accurate picture of just how dominant Coach Schembechler's teams were during his tenure.

Coach Schembechler's Conference Performance Statistics – 1969

Bo's numbers in his first season were very good on both sides of the ball. His point differential of plus twenty-four points per game was reminiscent of Bennie Oosterbaan's 1948 team. His team averaged thirty-five points per game which was an improvement of almost eight points per game from 1968. The Wolverines scored over fifty points in two games and over thirty in three more. They only scored twelve in their loss at Michigan State and were held to twenty-four points in the season finale against ohio state.

Defensively, the Wolverines were about four points better than the 1968 team so there were noticeable differences on both sides of the ball. It took Bo and his staff a couple of conference games to get the "bugs" out on defense as they allowed twenty and twenty-three points in their first two league games. After that, four straight conference foes failed to score more than ten points until the buckeyes managed to put twelve on the board in the last game of the season.

<u>Bo's Big Ten Performance Statistics – 1969</u>

Year*	Place	Games	Won-Lost-Tied	Scored/Avg.	Allowed/Avg.	+/- Difference
1969	1st (Tie)	7	6-1-0	245/35.0	77/11.0	+24.0

*Bold Year = Big Ten Championship Season

Michigan was an improved team in 1969, but the conference record was exactly the same with one big difference. The shocking upset win over the buckeyes would send the program in a new, and better, direction. Bo Schembechler's football teams established a new level of excellence that lasted for the next two decades!

Coach Schembechler's Conference Performance Statistics – 1970 to 1979

If you don't include ohio state, Bo was almost unbeatable in the conference during the 1970s. He was really, really good. He never lost more than two conference games in a single season until 1979. His winning percentage in the 1970's was a Yost-like winning rate of just over eight-seven percent (.873) percent – wow! Bo's Wolverines were the best team in the conference during the seventies, but Woody and his buckeyes were always nipping at Michigan's heels. Michigan was in position to challenge for the Big Ten title every year thanks to the great teams that Coach Schembechler put on the field from 1970 to 1979. Michigan and osu took their turns beating each other in this decade, but managed to defeat just about everyone else along the way.

When you look at the numbers, it is easy to understand why the Wolverines were so good from 1970 to 1979. On offense, Michigan averaged over thirty points per game for eight of the ten seasons in this decade. His 1976 team averaged just over thirty-four points (34.3) points per game which was the highest per game average for a season during this era. Eight teams in this decade averaged over thirty points per game. Only the 1972 team (20.2) and the 1974 (26.8) team failed to average over thirty points per game during the decade.

Bo's Big Ten Performance Statistics – 1970-1979

Year*	Place	Games	Won-Lost-Tied	Scored/Avg.	Allowed/Avg.	+/- Difference
1970	Tie 2nd	7	6-1-0	237/33.9	68/9.7	+24.2
1971	1st	8	8-0-0	269/33.6	70/8.8	+24.8
1972	Tie 1st	8	7-1-0	162/20.2	34/4.3	+15.9
1973	Tie 1st	8	7-0-1	245/30.6	58/7.3	+23.4
1974	Tie 1st	8	7-1-0	214/26.8	59/7.4	+19.4
1975	2nd	8	7-1-0	254/31.8	76/9.5	+22.3
1976	Tie 1st	8	7-1-0	274/34.3	67/8.4	+25.9
1977	Tie 1st	8	7-1-0	257/32.1	78/9.8	+22.3
1978	Tie 1st	8	7-1-0	261/32.6	57/7.1	+25.5
1979	3rd	8	6-2-0	245/30.6	105/13.1	+17.5
Totals	-------	**79**	**69-9-1**	**2418/30.6**	**672/8.5**	**+22.1**

*Bold Year = Big Ten Championship Season

It gets even better when you look at the defensive side of the ball where Bo made dramatic improvements from his first year at Michigan. In 1970 the Wolverines allowed an average of about ten points (9.7) per game and then improved on that number over the next two seasons and got it down to an average of just over four points (4.3) per game. It's very difficult to lose a game when you are only allowing four points a game, are you kidding? Nine of the ten teams of this decade allowed less than ten points per game with the 1979 team being the high mark (13.1 points allowed per game) for the decade. Bo's defense made it very difficult for their Big Ten opponents to score and that made it very difficult for Michigan to lose in the conference for the entire decade.

Bo's significant improvements on both sides of the ball produced some amazing point differentials and a ton of conference victories. Once again, the difference between points scored and points allowed were some of the highest numbers ever recorded in Michigan Football History. Only Fielding Yost did better for a significant period of time. Seven of Bo's teams in this era had point differentials of twenty or more points. The lowest point difference of the decade was just under sixteen points (+15.9) per game. Two teams, 1976 (+25.9) and 1978 (+25.5) had point differentials over twenty-five points and two more 1970 (+24.2) and 1971 (+24.8) had point differentials of just over twenty-four points per game. All of these numbers meant that the Wolverines were more than three touchdowns better than their Big Ten opponents for the decade. Wow!

Coach Schembechler's phenomenal numbers allowed him to co-own the Big Ten, along with his mentor, friend and chief rival, Woody Hayes, during the 1970s. Both teams were exceptional during this decade, but Bo and his Wolverines were better. Michigan won sixty-nine games, lost nine and tied one (69-9-1) during the seventies. His teams scored about thirty points per game and only allowed about nine points per contest. The point differential for the decade averaged over twenty-two points (+22.1) per game. No wonder the Wolverines won almost eighty-eight percent (.879) of their conference games from 1970 to 1979. Michigan was the best team in the Big Ten during the seventies – period.

Coach Schembechler's Conference Performance Statistics – 1980 to 1989

Since Bo set the bar very high in the seventies, it was hard to fathom another decade of such dominance. That's not to say he didn't try, but things were not quite as good for Coach Schembechler and his Wolverines in the eighties. However, there are nine other Big Ten teams that would have taken his record for this decade in a heartbeat! Michigan was a little more human in the Bo's last decade, but they were still very, very good.

The good news was that the Wolverines won enough games to win four conference titles and only had to share one championship during this decade (1986). He did have three undefeated conference seasons (1980, 1988 and 1989), but also had the only four-loss season of his tenure in 1984 and also lost three conference games in 1987. Bo continued to dominate the other conference teams, but experienced five more defeats (14 losses in the 1980s compared to 9 losses in the 1970s) than he did in the seventies. The Wolverines still put up some incredible numbers on both sides of the ball in the eighties. They just were not as dominating as they were during the seventies.

Once again, the numbers really help to explain what happened to Michigan Football during the eighties. There was a slight decline in offensive productivity (29.1 points per game), but still not as good as in the seventies (30.6 points per game). Bo's Wolverines were more "beatable" during the eighties, but not that much. On offense, Michigan averaged over thirty points per game for six of the ten seasons in this decade. His 1988 team averaged just over thirty-four points (34.1) points per game which was the second highest per game average for his twenty-one-year tenure. Every team of the decade averaged over twenty-five points per game except the injury plagued team of 1984 which struggled to average eighteen points per game.

Bo's Big Ten Performance Statistics – 1980-1989

Year*	Place	Games	Won-Lost-Tied	Scored/Avg.	Allowed/Avg.	+/-Difference
1980	1st	8	8-0-0	220/27.5	64/8.0	+19.5
1981	Tie 3rd	9	6-3-0	267/29.7	125/13.9	+15.8
1982	1st	9	8-1-0	273/30.3	126/14.0	+16.3
1983	2nd	9	8-1-0	304/33.8	109/12.1	+21.6
1984	Tie 6th	9	5-4-0	164/18.2	142/15.8	+2.4
1985	2nd	8	6-1-1	241/30.1	60/7.5	+22.6
1986	Tie 1st	8	7-1-0	262/32.8	118/14.8	+18.0
1987	4th	8	5-3-0	203/25.4	104/13.0	+12.4
1988	1st	8	7-0-1	273/34.1	94/11.8	+22.3
1989	1st	8	8-0-0	241/30.1	99/12.4	+17.7
Totals	------	84	68-14-2	2448/29.1	1041/12.4	+16.7

*Bold Year = Big Ten Championship Season

Once again, the numbers really help to explain what happened to Michigan Football during the eighties. There was a slight decline in offensive productivity (29.1 points per game), but still not as good as in the seventies (30.6 points per game). Bo's Wolverines were more "beatable" during the eighties, but not that much. On offense, Michigan averaged over thirty points per game for six of the ten seasons in this decade. His 1988 team averaged just over thirty-four points (34.1) points per game which was the second highest per game average for his Michigan career.

As I have already mentioned, the biggest decline took place on the defensive side of the ball. Only two teams allowed less than ten points per game (1980 & 1985) as opposed to nine teams who accomplished this feat in the seventies. The Wolverines only allowed an average of about nine points (8.5) per game in the seventies, but saw that number jump (by Bo's standards) to over twelve points per game (12.5) in the eighties. No, the sky was not falling, but Bo's teams allowed more points and scored slightly less which helps to explain why his overall record slipped a little in the last ten years of his Michigan coaching tenure.

Even though Bo's point differentials remained very positive in the eighties they were not as good as the ones his teams achieved in the seventies. However, they were still good enough to allow the Wolverines to win a ton of Big Ten games in the last decade of Bo's Michigan coaching gig. Coach Schembechler's last ten teams had three seasons with positive point differentials greater than twenty-one points (1983, 1985, 1988). His 1985 and 1988 teams both posted point differentials of plus twenty-two points per game which were the highest numbers achieved in the eighties. Every team, except the 1984 team, had a positive point differential of at least twelve points. The lowest point difference of the decade was just over plus two points per game (+2.4) which was also the worst differential of Bo's tenure. When the decade of the eighties was over, the Wolverines had finished with a very positive point differential of over sixteen points (+16.7) per conference game. You won't lose too many games in any league with those numbers!

Coach Schembechler's teams continued to perform at a very high level in their conference games during the eighties. Bo's teams were usually picked to be in contention for Big Ten title and his Wolverines rarely disappointed Bo or the fans. Michigan won sixty-eight games, lost fourteen and tied two (68-14-2) during the eighties. Coach Schembechler's eighties teams scored about thirty points per game (29.1) and only allowed about twelve (12.4) points per contest. The point differential for the decade averaged over plus sixteen points (+16.7) per game. Overall, these exceptional numbers allowed the Wolverines to win about eighty-two percent (.821) of their conference games from 1980 to 1989. This was a performance decline of about six percent compared to the seventies, but everybody else in the Big Ten would have been very happy with these numbers and that's a fact!

Coach Schembechler's Conference Performance Statistical Summary 1969-1989

Bo's twenty-one year Big Ten tenure was the third longest in conference history. Only Amos Alanzo Stagg (37 years) and Woody Hayes (28 years) coached in the conference longer than Schembechler. Bo's teams were simply amazing from 1969 to 1989. Bo prepared his teams to beat ohio state, win the conference championship and play in the Rose Bowl every year. In the end, his teams didn't accomplish all of those lofty goals every season, but they came very close. Bo jump started the Michigan Football Program when he arrived in 1969 and he didn't stop energizing his Wolverine Football teams for twenty-one years. Michigan had ceased to be a threat in the conference since the early fifties. Bo fixed that problem by creating a team that stood shoulder to shoulder with the buckeyes and above everyone else in the Big Ten conference.

The Schembechler Era- A Final Look at the Key Big Ten Statistics

Year(s)	Games	Won-Lost-Tied	Scored/Avg.	Allowed/Avg.	+/- Difference
1969	7	6-1-0	245/35.0	77/11.0	+24.0
1970s	79	69-9-1	2418/30.6	672/8.5	+22.1
1980s	84	68-14-2	2448/29.1	1041/12.4	+16.7
Totals	**170**	**143-24-3**	**5111/30.1**	**1790/10.5**	**+19.6**

When it was all said and done, Bo coached in a total of one hundred and seventy Big Ten Football games. He won one hundred and forty-three of those games, lost twenty-four and tied three (143-24-3). Coach Schembechler's teams were stellar on both sides of the ball for twenty-one years. His offenses averaged just over thirty-points per game (30.1) and his defenses made it extremely hard to score (10.5 points allowed per game) and win against Michigan. His point differential was almost plus twenty points per game (+19.6) which means he blew out a lot of conference teams during his tenure. His winning percentage worked out to an astonishing rate of over eighty-five percent (.850) which is the best in conference history! His home winning percentage as well as his achievements on the road also worked out to be conference standards. Nobody did the Big Ten better than Bo, ever! Got it?

Conference Championships

Bo came to Ann Arbor to do three things: 1) Beat ohio state, 2) Win the Big Ten Conference Championship and 3) Win the Rose Bowl every year – that was it. Bo tried to keep things simple so if you could count to three (and get into Michigan), you could play for Bo. As I mentioned in

Chapter Two, "balance" was the word that described the state of the Big Ten Conference from 1948 to 1968. The "Big Two and Little Eight" was how people described the conference during the Bo Era. As we just learned, Michigan posted the most conference wins during this period and those wins translated into thirteen conference titles. Michigan won five Big Ten Championships and tied for eight more. The buckeyes were second with four titles and shared eight others (seven with Michigan). Bo and Woody pretty much "bullied" the rest of the conference from 1969 to 1978. After Woody left Bo kept winning (four more titles and a share of another) and everybody else did their best to stay in the hunt.

The chart below provides a breakdown of how the conference championships were distributed from 1969 to 1989: Of course, Michigan and ohio state dominated during this period, didn't they?

School	Total	Titles	Shared	Years (T = Tied for the Championship - 1 or more team)
Michigan	**13**	**5**	**8**	**1969 (T), 1971, 1972 (T), 1973 (T), 1974 (T), 1976 (T)** **1977 (T), 1978 (T), 1980, 1982, 1986 (T), 1988, 1989**
osu	12	4	8	1969 (T), 1970, 1972 (T), 1973 (T), 1974 (T), 1975 1976 (T), 1977 (T), 1979, 1981 (T), 1984, 1986 (T)
MSU	2	1	1	1978 (T), 1987
Illinois	1	1	0	1983
Iowa	2	1	1	1981 (T), 1985

Again, the Big Two won or shared eighteen of the twenty-one conference titles in the Bo Era. Only three teams during this time period won outright championships (Illinois-1983, Iowa 1985 and Michigan State-1987). That was it – everything else was about the Wolverines and the buckeyes. Michigan was very consistent during the Bo Era – when they weren't winning or sharing the title they were close to the top. Bo's worst conference finish was a tie for sixth in the 1984 season. Otherwise, he was always in the upper third of the conference and challenging for the championship. The chart below compares Michigan's conference finishes from the Pre-Bo Era to the Bo Era:

Place	Pre-Bo Era	Bo Era
First	4 (1 Tied)	13 (8 Tied)
Second	3 (1 Tied)	4 (1 tied)
Third	2 (1 Tied)	2 (1 Tied)
Fourth	2 (1 Tied)	1
Fifth	4 (4 Tied)	0
Sixth	2	1 (Tied)
Seventh	2 (1 Tied)	0
Eighth	1	0
Ninth	0	0
Tenth	1	0

Bo's Wolverines were the model of excellence and consistency during his tenure. Seventeen of his teams finished in the top two spots in the Big Ten in twenty-one years. He had two third place finishes and one sixth place season. That's it! Everyone expected Michigan to be among the best teams in the conference and rarely did Bo disappoint them!

Bo vs the Big Ten

Bo's numbers are even more impressive when you examine how they broke down against each conference team. Michigan had losing records against three conference teams in the Oosterbaan-Elliott Era (MSU, osu, and Purdue). So, Bo knew he had some work to do when he arrived in addition to beating the buckeyes. The Wolverines needed to play better against everybody in the conference and that's exactly what they did!

The chart that follows shows how Michigan did in the Big Ten before he arrived and during his tenure. He made significant improvements against every team. However, his numbers against Northwestern, Indiana, Minnesota and Wisconsin were amazing. Nobody in the Big Ten looked forward to playing Michigan from 1969 to 1989, I guarantee it!

Oosterbaan-Elliott Era - 1948-1968   Schembechler Era – 1969-1989

Team	Won	Lost	Tied	Win %	Team	Won	Lost	Tied	Win %
Illinois	13	8	0	.620	Illinois	19	1	1	.930
Indiana	11	4	0	.730	Indiana	16	1	0	.940
Iowa	6	2	2	.700	Iowa	13	3	1	.790
Michigan State	4	10	1	.300	Michigan State	17	4	0	.810
Minnesota	12	8	1	.600	Minnesota	19	2	0	.905
Northwestern	14	5	0	.740	Northwestern	14	0	0	1.000
ohio state	8	12	1	.405	ohio state	11	9	1	.550
Purdue	4	5	1	.450	Purdue	16	3	0	.840
Wisconsin	5	3	0	.630	Wisconsin	18	1	0	.950
Totals	77	57	6	.570	Totals	143	24	3	.850

Bo's teams played better, a lot better, in the Big Ten than in the Pre-Bo Era. His Big Ten and ohio state pedigree paid big dividends for Canham and the rest of Wolverine Nation. Coach Schembechler's teams made dramatic improvements in Michigan's performance against every conference team. Of course, his epic battles with Woody were described as the "Ten Year War" and always came down to a final confrontation for the Big Ten Championship. Bo and his Wolverines set the standard for the conference from 1969 to 1989 and it was a very high standard indeed!

When Bo left the sidelines after the 1989 season he was the Dean of Big Ten coaches and he was also a survivor. He coached for twenty-one years and faced off against forty-two different men who represented the other nine conference teams. Bo's twenty-one-year run gave Michigan a level of stability that no other conference team enjoyed during this era.

Schembechler's program was in place and only required some minor tweaks over the years. This is one of the key reasons that Michigan was so difficult to beat during this era. The dominance of Michigan and ohio state during this period made the Big Ten a "grave yard" for a lot of coaches who failed to turn their programs around from 1969 to 1989. Here is a look at the number of coaches who coached at each conference school during Bo Schembechler's tenure at Michigan.

Team	Coaches	Team	Coaches
Illinois	5	Northwestern	5
Indiana	4	ohio state	3
Iowa	4	Purdue	6
Michigan State	5	Wisconsin	5
Minnesota	5	**Total**	42

Forty-two coaches came and went during Coach Schembechler's tenure at Michigan! That is an amazing statistic. Bo's numbers were not just good, they were exceptional for a significant length of time. So, he made life difficult for a lot of other good men. Only the legendary Fielding Yost sustained such a high winning rate for such a long time.

Bo Schembechler definitely put Michigan Football back on the national radar and his efforts enhanced the legacy of the "Champions of the West" and launched what many experts call the "modern era" of Michigan Football. Coaches like Fielding H. Yost and Glenn E. Schembechler don't come around very often, but Michigan was extremely fortunate to have them both!

All-Conference Players

Bo knew he had to recruit more great players and more good players if he was going to turn things around in Ann Arbor so that's exactly what he did. Again, Bo wasn't a big fan of the recruiting process, but he was very good at it. As a result, Bo recruited some of the best players in the country and they ensured that significant improvements were made at the corner of Main Street and Stadium Boulevard in Ann Arbor.

It would be a huge understatement to say that Bo made a positive difference between the All-Conference selections in the Pre-Bo Era and the Bo Era. What he did to recruit and develop quality players at Michigan was simply amazing. According to the Bentley Historical Library, a total of forty-two Michigan Men earned fifty-two All-Conference selections from 1948 to

1968. In the next twenty-one years, Bo coached ninety-seven players who earned a total of one hundred thirty-nine first team conference selections. If Darth Vader would have seen this stat, he would have said, "Impressive, most impressive!"

Bo had at least two All-Conference players every season, even in the underachieving 1984 campaign. He had eleven first team selections in 1970 and came close with ten in 1980. He also had nine all-Conference players in 1976. It worked out to an average of almost seven (6.62) All-Conference players per year.

Bo recruited and coached Mark Messner, Michigan's first ever four-time All-Conference player, who played from 1985 through 1988. He also had three Wolverines who earned conference recognition for three consecutive years. (Dave Brown 1972-74, Rick Leach 1976-78, and Anthony Carter 1980-82). Finally, he also had thirty-six players who earned back to back first team conference honors from 1969 to 1989.

Summary

Overall, Bo found a lot of outstanding players who wanted to play for the Maize and Blue. And, oh how they played. When it was all said and done, the Bo Era saw Michigan rise again to the top of the Big Ten Conference and remain there for a very long time. They were talented, tough and they knew how to beat the buckeyes and everybody else in the conference. Bo said he would coach "his way" when he got to Michigan and "his way" worked out just fine. I don't know if the other coaches in the Big Ten had a party when Bo retired, but they should have – they must have been very happy to see him go.

Big Ten Conference Statistical Comparison – 1948 to 1989

Category	1948-1968	1969-1989
Conference Championships	3	5
Shared Conference Championships	1	8
Conference Championship Drought	14 (1951-1964)	4 (1983-1986)
Number of Wining Conference Seasons	11	21
Number of Losing Conference Seasons	7	0
Number of Even Conference Seasons	3	0
Total Conference Games Played	140	170
Conference Wins	77	143
Conference Losses	57	24
Conference Ties	6	3
Conference Winning %	.570	.850
Total Conference Home Games	87	87
Conference Home Wins	53	78
Conference Home Losses	30	8
Conference Home Ties	4	3
Conference Home Winning %	.630	.910
Total Conference Road Games	53	83
Conference Road Wins	24	65
Conference Road Losses	27	16
Conference Road Ties	2	2
Conference Road Winning %	.470	.795
Number of All-Conference Players	42	97
Number of All-Conference Selections	52	139

BO DID NOT RECRUIT HIS FIRST CAPTAIN, BUT JIM MANDICH PROVED HIMSELF TO BE
AN OUTSTANDING LEADER FOR BO'S FIRST FOOTBALL TEAM IN 1969.

CHAPTER THREE
BO AND NOTRE DAME

BO MADE IT very clear during his first press conference that he was hired to beat ohio state. He knew that he wouldn't last very long as the head coach at Michigan if he didn't get that situation turned around. He intended to get it done sooner than later and that's exactly what he did. One important lesson he learned in that first year was that the team from East Lansing was also important. Maybe Bo underestimated the intensity of the MSU rivalry, but he vowed that his Wolverines would be better prepared against future Spartan football teams and they were!

Coach Schembechler knew about rivalries from his time at ohio state, especially about the team "up north," but now he was coaching the team "up north" and he knew that his former coach and mentor, Woody Hayes, had him in his sights. The Spartans would get on his radar very quickly. Minnesota had even been a challenge for the Wolverines in the previous ten years so there was lots of work to be done against the "rivals." The Wolverines hadn't played Notre Dame since 1943, but Michigan's sports "Marketing Marvel," aka Don Canham, would change that in time. He was all about filling Michigan Stadium so he set out to get the Irish on the schedule as soon as he could make it happen.

Let's take a closer look at how Bo's teams did against Michigan's "Big Four" – the rivals that matter just a little more, ok, some of them a lot more. I will stick to the same sequence that I used in Chapter Three to examine Bo's performance against Michigan's very special rivals.

Michigan and Notre Dame – The Bo Era 1969-1977

When Don Canham took over as Athletic Director in 1968, the Michigan-Notre Dame rivalry had not played out on the field for twenty-four years. Canham knew this natural rivalry would be a great draw at Michigan Stadium so he negotiated with the Irish AD Moose Krause to get both teams back on the same field. Even though Canham and Krause came to an agreement in 1970, scheduling commitments prevented an immediate resumption of the series. Finally, Michigan and Notre Dame made room on their schedules for a game on September 23, 1978. It was supposed to be a match-up of two great programs and two great friends Bo and Ara – college teammates. Ara spoiled the personal matchup drama, by retiring from Notre Dame after the 1974 season.

From 1969 to 1977, Michigan and Notre Dame continued their competition off the field. During this period, the Wolverines posted a record of eighty-six wins, thirteen losses and three ties (86-13-3) during this period. That worked out to an excellent winning rate of almost eighty-six percent (.858). The Irish were also doing some winning during this stretch and managed to post some very impressive numbers for their program. How about eighty-three wins, seventeen losses and one tie (83-17-1) for a winning percentage of just under eighty-three percent (.827)? Yes, both teams were good during the nine years that preceded the renewal of this legendary rivalry.

Although Michigan had the edge in games won and winning percentage during this period, Notre Dame won two national championships – Parseghian won his second in 1973 and Dan Devine won his first in 1977. Michigan was rated in the top nine teams in the country every year from 1969 to 1977. Notre Dame was rated in the top thirteen teams in eight of the nine years of this period. They were not ranked in 1975, Dan Devine's first year, despite a respectable record of eight victories and only three defeats.

On the All-American front, Michigan had twenty-two All-Americans selections from 1969 to 1977. Notre Dame was just a little bit better here with a total of twenty-four All-American picks during the same period. Neither team had a Heisman Trophy winner during this time. Overall, both teams were back in the conversation when the discussion was about the top programs in the country.

Michigan and Notre Dame – The Bo Era 1978--1989

Michigan and Notre Dame were literally at the top of their games when they finally met in South Bend on September 23, 1978. The Irish, under Dan Devine, were defending National Champions having won the title in 1977 with a dominating victory (38-10) over Texas in the Cotton Bowl (Final record was (11-1-0). Bo's Wolverines finished 1977 with a record of ten wins and two losses (10-2-0) and a share of the Big Ten Championship. Finally, after thirty-four years, Michigan and Notre Dame would again do battle on the football field.

The Irish, who had been upset in the first game of the season by Missouri, started well against the Wolverines and led by seven points (14-7) at halftime. Bo must have said all the right things during the mid-game break as the Maize and Blue footballers outscored Notre Dame in the second half. The Wolverines walked off the field with a hard-earned victory (28-14).

Bo lost the next two to Devine and his Fighting Irish during the 1979 and 1980 seasons. In 1981 new coach Gerry Faust led his top ranked Irish into Michigan Stadium to face the eleventh ranked Wolverines, who had been upset in the season opener by Wisconsin. Bo's team had something to prove and they made a strong statement with a decisive win (25-7) against the Golden Domers. In 1982 Faust and his Notre Dame footballers hosted Michigan in the first night game in Irish football history. The Irish got the best of the Wolverines that night in a close game (Irish 23 and Wolverines 17).

Scheduling commitments led to a two-year break in 1983 and 1984 so the series didn't resume again until 1985. The unranked Wolverines hosted a thirteenth ranked Irish team on September 14, 1985. Michigan won the game (20-12) and finished with a record of ten wins, one loss and one tie (10-1-1) for the season. The 1986 game in South Bend marked a reunion of sorts when two friends, Bo and Lou Holtz, met as opponents for the first time. Lou's game plan gave Bo and his defense fits, but the Wolverines earned a narrow one-point victory (24-23). Michigan's back to back wins in 1985 and 1986 were sweet, but Lou would turn the tables on Bo for the next three years.

Notre Dame won handily in 1987 (26-7) and Lou's Irish came back with a narrow victory (19-17) in 1988 when Mike Gillette missed a 48-yard field goal attempt on the final play of the game. Bo's last game against Notre Dame in 1989 was memorable, but not in a good way. The second ranked Wolverines outplayed the top-ranked Irish at the line of scrimmage. However,

Rocket Ismail returned two straight second half kickoffs for touchdowns and put the game out of reach (Final Score ND 24 – UM 19).

Here is a breakdown of the key statistics for the renewal of the Michigan vs Notre Dame series during the Post-Bo Era:

Year	Home Team	Rankings	Winner	Score	Attendance
1978	Notre Dame	UM #5-ND #14	UM	28-14	59,075
1979	Michigan	UM #6-ND #9	ND	10-12	105,111
1980	Notre Dame	UM #14-ND #8	ND	27-29	59,075
1981	Michigan	UM #11-ND #1	UM	25-7	105,888
1982	Notre Dame	UM #10-ND #20	ND	17-23	59,075
1985	Michigan	UM/NR-ND #13	UM	20-12	105,523
1986	Notre Dame	UM #3-ND/NR	UM	24-23	59,075
1987	Michigan	UM #9-ND #16	ND	7-26	106,098
1988	Notre Dame	UM #9-ND #13	ND	17-19	59,075
1989	Michigan	UM #2-ND #1	ND	19-24	105,912

The Wolverines and the Irish played a total of ten games during the Bo Era. Michigan won four of the first seven games, but lost the last three. At least one team was ranked in the top twenty teams and eight times both teams were ranked. Three times both were ranked in the top ten and once, in 1989, Number Two Michigan hosted the Top Ranked Irish. Every game was intense, most were close and many were instant classics. The Michigan-Notre Dame game was more like an early season bowl game because of the impact it usually had on the national rankings. It became much more than a non-conference tune up for Michigan, not quite the "Ten Year War," but very intense.

Every game was a sell-out which made Canham, Krause, and their predecessors smile. The Wolverines averaged over one hundred and six thousand fans (106,706) for the five games played at Michigan Stadium so Don Canham's instincts were correct. He knew that this non-conference game would be a great attraction and he was right. Although Bo understood the importance of the game, he always felt it was a distraction that took away from the conference schedule.

Maybe it made his job just a little more difficult from the "strength of schedule" standpoint, but that's the life of the Head Football Coach at The University of Michigan.

Here is a chart that shows how the teams compared during the twenty-one seasons of the Bo Era:

Category	Michigan	Notre Dame
Total Wins	194	175
Total Losses	48	63
Total Ties	3	3
Winning Percentage	.796	.732
# Winning Seasons	20	18
# Losing Seasons	0	3
# Even Seasons	1	0
National Championships	0	1
Top Ten Poll Rankings	16	9
Seasons – Not ranked	2	8
Heisman Trophy Winners	0	1
All-American Selections	44	42

At the end of the Bo Era the total wins for both storied programs looked like this: Michigan started this era with five hundred and nine total wins and Bo's one hundred ninety-four victories pushed the total to seven hundred and three (703) program victories. The Irish began the Bo Era with a total of five hundred and eight victories and their one hundred and seventy-five wins during the Bo Era resulted in a new total of six hundred and eighty-three (683) total wins.

Unlike the twenty-one years before Bo arrived, Michigan did not lose twenty-three games in comparison to the Irish, they gained nineteen. Both teams were good during the Pre-Bo Era, but the Wolverines were better. Michigan now had twenty more program wins than the Irish. Bo definitely returned the Maize and Blue to the national football conversation and there was little doubt about which Division I program had the most overall wins.

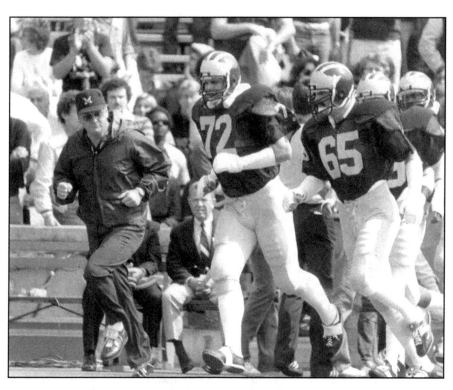

BO, ALONG WITH FUTURE ALL-AMERICANS KURT BECKER (#72) AND ED MURANSKY (#65),
LEADS THE WOLVERINES ONTO THE FIELD AGAINST # 1 RANKED NOTRE DAME ON 09-19-1981.
THE ELEVENTH RANKED WOLVERINES BEAT THE IRISH THAT DAY BY A SCORE OF 25-7.

CHAPTER FOUR

BO AND MINNESOTA

MICHIGAN'S OVERALL RECORD against Minnesota during the Pre-Bo Era was twelve wins, eight losses and one tie (12-8-1). However, the Gophers had won six of the nine most recent games. Bo had already lost his first "rival" game at Michigan State. He certainly didn't want to repeat that performance at Minnesota in late-October. As it turned out, Bo got off to a great start against Minnesota and he kept things under control for most of his twenty-one years at Michigan. It was a "one-sided" rivalry most of the time, but the Gophers did sneak up on the Wolverines a few times. And, when they did, it was really painful for Bo and Michigan Nation! Let's see how Coach Schembechler fared against the Golden Gophers and the men who coached at Minnesota from 1969 to 1989.

Bo Schembechler and Murray Warmath 1969-1971

Murray Warmath was a winner at Minnesota. He won two Big Ten Titles and one national championship from 1954 to 1968. Warmath posted a record of 1 win and 4 losses against Bennie Oosterbaan, but did much better against Bump Elliott. Murray Warmath posted 6 wins and 4 losses against Michigan during the Elliott Era. So, he knew what he was doing against Michigan. Bo was not going to take this game lightly. I guess Bo wanted to send a message in his first game against Minnesota which was the sixtieth game in the series. It wasn't even close as the Wolverines defeated the Gophers by twenty-six points (35-9). Minnesota was unable to sneak up on Michigan this time, or just about any other time for that matter.

So, Bo made sure the Little Brown Jug returned to Ann Arbor, as planned. Things didn't get any easier for Coach Warmath during the next two games against Michigan. Bo's Boys won in 1970 by a score of 39-13 and posted another lopsided win (35-7) in 1971. Warmath wasn't doing very well against anybody else either. He finally left the Minnesota sidelines after going 4-7-0 in 1971.

Coach Schembechler's program was on the rise at the same time that Minnesota was falling. Check out the chart below to see how both coaches did with their programs during the early Schembechler Era.

Michigan and Minnesota Program Summaries 1969-1971

Coach	Games*	Won-Lost-Tied	Win %	B10 Games	W-L-T	Win %
Bo	33	28-5-0	.848	22	20-2-0	.909
Warmath	31	11-18-2	.387	22	9-12-1	.432

*Note – These numbers include all bowl games that each team played in from 1969 to 1971

Bo had the edge over Murray Warmath's Gophers in every category from 1969 to 1971. He more than doubled Minnesota's total and did the same in conference play. Michigan posted three winning seasons during this period, but the Gophers didn't post any. Both teams were still members of the Big Ten Conference during this time, but Michigan played like they were in a different league. Bo led his team to two conference titles in three years while the Gophers won none. Coach Schembechler's teams were now part of the Big Ten's "Big Two" while the Warmath's Gophers slipped to the bottom third of the "Little Eight."

Coach Schembechler vs Coach Warmath 1969-1971

Bo was a quick study. He could connect the dots faster than a lot of other coaches. After his shaky start in his first "rivalry game" against Duffy's Spartans Bo figured things pretty quickly. Yes, Ohio State was always going to be the biggest game of the season, but the Paul Bunyan Trophy and the Little Brown Jug required a special focus as well. Bo defeated Murray Warmath and his Gophers three straight games and the games weren't that close. Take a look at the numbers below to see what happened in the three matchups between Bo Schembechler and Murray Warmath.

Head-to-Head Summary 1969-1971

Games	Won-Lost-Tied	Win %	Scored/Avg.	Allowed/Avg.	+/- Difference
Home	1-0-0	1.000	39/39.0	13/13.0	+26.0
Away	2-0-0	1.000	70/35.0	16.8.0	+27.0
Totals	**3-0-0**	**1.000**	**109/36.3**	**29/9.7**	**+26.6**

Yes, the numbers tell the story. Michigan was a much better team than Minnesota when they faced each other from 1969 to 1971. Bo was on a "roll" and Coach Warmath was starting to slide down a very slippery slope that would end with his departure in 1971. Murray Warmath had a very good run while he was at Minnesota. He left with a winning record, but his best years were definitely behind him. Sadly, for Gopher Fans, Bo's arrival was the beginning of the end for Murray Warmath's time in Minneapolis. Something would have to change if the Gophers ever hoped to recapture the Little Brown Jug from Schembechler and his Wolverines.

Bo Schembechler and Cal Stoll 1972-1978

Minnesota hired an energetic man named Calvin C. "Cal" Stoll to breathe life back into the failing Gopher Football program starting in 1972. Stoll had head coaching experience after a three-year run at Wake Forest and he knew about Michigan and the Big Ten. Cal Stoll played for the Gophers and coached at Michigan State for ten years under Duffy Daugherty. Gopher fans were hoping that Cal Stoll was the man who could do for Minnesota what Bo Schembechler was doing at Michigan.

As it turned out, Bo didn't show any mercy to his new Big Ten protégé. Bo feasted on the Gophers in Stoll's first game in 1972. Michigan blasted Minnesota by a score of 42-0 in Stoll's Little Brown Jug debut. Michigan's Homecoming crowd loved it, but Stoll probably didn't like it very much. Yes, there was a lot of work to be done in Minnesota, if they were going to win the "Jug" anytime soon.

Cal Stoll kept working hard and made some improvements in the Minnesota Football program. He posted winning seasons in three out of four years (1973-1976), but he really never challenged for the Big Ten Title. Cal Stoll produced four winning seasons in seven years at

Minnesota, but it wasn't good enough. Although he was able to beat Bo once, he didn't do it often enough. Here is a look at how the two coaches and their programs compared during the bulk of the Seventies.

Michigan and Minnesota Program Summaries 1972-1978

Coach	Games*	Won-Lost-Tied	Win %	B10 Games	W-L-T	Win %
Bo	81	68-10-3	.858	56	49-6-1	.883
Stoll	78	39-39-0	.500	56	27-29-0	.482

*Note – These numbers include all bowl games that each team played in from 1972 to 1978

Again, Bo had the edge over Cal Stoll in every category from 1972 to 1978. Bo's Wolverines had a lot more wins and a lot less defeats. Bo had one of the best records in the 1970s and Minnesota did not. The Wolverines posted seven-consecutive ten-win seasons and won at least seven Big Ten games every year. Minnesota had two seven-win seasons, but only managed to win six Big Ten games once in 1973.

Michigan won, or shared, six conference titles during this period while Minnesota had two third place finishes. The rest of the time they were in the bottom half of the league standings. Bottom line – the Wolverines were still at the elite level in conference play while the Gophers were struggling to stay out of last place. Cal Stoll had a decent run at Minnesota, but he didn't win enough games against Bo and the rest of the conference. It was time for a change in 1978.

Coach Schembechler vs Coach Stoll 1972-1978

Bo, and Michigan, continued to "own" the Gophers from 1972 to 1976. Schembechler's winning streak against Minnesota reached eight games after his win in 1976. The 1977 game saw the #1 ranked Wolverines travel to Minnesota for their annual battle for the Little Brown Jug. The game was supposed to be played on grass, but the two teams slugged it out on a green, brown, muddy mess of a field. Michigan's triple option attack ran out of options as the Gophers stopped them cold.

The Gophers stunned the Wolverines with a shutout victory (16-0) and knocked them off the top of the rankings. Yes, the Minnesota "mudders" shut out the top team in the country that day. As John Falk reported in his great book, "*If These Walls Could Talk*," the Minnesota grounds-keeper "forgot" to turn off the water from the previous evening. It wasn't turned off until Falk showed up at 6:00 am to sound the alarm. Falk wrote that he "was "suspicious of the incident, but nothing could be proved." Chalk it up to the home field advantage – you win some, you lose some, and sometimes you "steal" one. In this case re-sodding the field at the end of the season was a fair price to pay for a victory over Michigan. Minnesota was happy to keep the Little Brown Jug in Minneapolis for a year. Yes, very happy!

The 1977 "upset" turned out to be the "high water mark" for Cal Stoll's football program. It went down as one of the greatest wins in Minnesota Football history. That huge win helped the Gophers finish the 1977 season with a record of 7 wins and 5 losses. Stoll coached the Gophers for one more year and then he was gone. Cal Stoll produced four winning seasons in seven years at Minnesota, but it wasn't good enough. Let's see how the two coaches did when they faced off against each other in seven Little Brown Jug games.

Head-to-Head Summary 1972-1978

Games	Won-Lost-Tied	Win %	Scored/Avg.	Allowed/Avg.	+/- Difference
Home	4-0-0	1.000	178/44.5	10/2.5	+42.0
Away	2-1-0	.667	66/22.0	44/14.6	+7.4
Totals	**6-1-0**	**.857**	**244/34.9**	**54/7.7**	**+27.2**

The numbers on the chart above tell a "happy" story for Wolverine fans and a "sad" tale for Gopher fans. Bo Schembechler coached his Wolverines to eight straight wins over the Gophers from 1969 to 1976. Minnesota's upset win in 1977, put an end to Bo's eight game winning streak over the Gophers. However, Bo came back with another win in 1978 and that was it for Cal Stoll. Once again, the numbers indicate just how dominant Schembechler's teams were in the Little Brown Jug series. The Gophers were only able to secure the trophy once during Cal Stoll's tenure. Otherwise, the "Jug" was in Ann Arbor most of the time which is how Bo and all the fine folks in Ann Arbor liked it!

Bo Schembechler and Joe Salem 1979-1983

Joseph N. "Smokey Joe" Salem was the next man up for the Minnesota Gophers. It was his job to build a winning program and beat Minnesota's rivals, especially Michigan. It was pretty clear what he had to accomplish in Minneapolis. The only question was, "Could he do it?" Joe Salem played quarterback for Murray Warmath from 1958-1960. He was part of some very good Gopher teams, including the National Championship team in 1960. He knew what the Big Ten was all about, so he seemed like the ideal man to turn around the Minnesota Football program.

Joe Salem's first encounter with Bo Schembechler's Wolverines did not go well. Michigan won in Ann Arbor by a score of 31-21. Of course, it was better than the 42-0 shutout in 1978, but it was still a loss and the "Jug" remained in Ann Arbor after the game. Joe Salem won nine games in his first two seasons and came up with a winning season in 1981 (6-5-0). However, he only won four games in the last two years so Joe Salem's time in Minneapolis came to an end after the 1983 season.

Michigan continued to be the better team from 1979 to 1983, a much better team. Check out the numbers to see how each coach fared during the Salem Years at Minnesota.

Michigan and Minnesota Program Summaries 1979-1983

Coach	Games*	Won-Lost-Tied	Win %	B10 Games	W-L-T	Win %
Bo	60	44-16-0	.733	43	36-7-0	.837
Salem	55	19-35-1	.356	45	12-32-1	.278

*Note – These numbers include all bowl games that each team played in from 1979 to 1983

Once again, Bo's program at Michigan was far better than Joe's was at Minnesota. Coach Schembechler had his system in place and it was working very well. Salem was trying to build something special and it just didn't work out! The numbers tell another dominant story as Bo's teams more than doubled Joe's win totals. Coach Schembechler also had less than half as many losses during this time so Michigan was doing a lot of things right while Minnesota couldn't get it right.

Bo Schembechler's Wolverines continued to have the advantage in Big Ten play and it was by a large margin of about 3 to 4 wins per season. Michigan won, or shared, three conference titles during this period. But, the Gophers best effort was a fifth-place finish in 1980. So, yes, the two programs were at opposite ends of the conference standings most of the time. Michigan was competing for the championship almost every season with Ohio State and the Gophers were just trying to get in the top half of the Big Ten title race every year. Bottom line – the Wolverines were still at the elite level in conference play while the Gophers were just trying to get better.

Coach Schembechler vs Coach Salem 1979-1983

Bo won all five of his games against Joe Salem's Minnesota team. He was perfect at home and away. Actually, his Wolverines were more dominant against the Gophers in Minneapolis than they were in Ann Arbor. The closest game was the ten-point loss (31-21) that Minnesota absorbed in 1979. After that, every game had a victory margin of at least twenty-one points. The worst defeat that Bo inflicted on Salem's Gophers was a 58-10 thrashing in his last game between the coaches in 1983.

Michigan was clearly the better team in every matchup from 1979 to 1983. Bo was always ready for the Gophers and Salem couldn't find a way to "sneak up" on the Wolverines. The Michigan Wolverines made winning against Minnesota a habit. It was a habit that Joe Salem could not break.

Head-to-Head Summary 1979-1983

Games	Won-Lost-Tied	Win %	Scored/Avg.	Allowed/Avg.	+/- Difference
Home	2-0-0	1.000	83/41.5	35/17.5	+24.0
Away	3-0-0	1.000	129/43.0	37/12.3	+30.7
Totals	5-0-0	1.000	212/42.5	72/14.4	+28.1

By the end of the 1983 season, it was clear that Joe Salem was not going to beat Michigan or take Minnesota to a Big Ten Title anytime soon. So, the Minnesota administrators went looking for a miracle worker to change the Gopher Football fortunes. Would Minnesota ever find a man who could beat Schembechler and Michigan along with the rest of the Big Ten teams?

Bo Schembechler and Lou Holtz 1984-1985

Although he was not known as a "miracle worker," Lou Holtz had a reputation for building winning college football programs. He also was an amateur magician. Hopefully, he could do some "magic" for the Gopher Football program and make Michigan's winning ways against Minnesota disappear! Although it was not common knowledge at the time, Holtz had a clause in his contract that if the Notre Dame job ever came open, he wanted to be a candidate, no matter how long he had been at Minnesota. So, Lou Holtz was living in Minnesota and committed to improving the Minnesota Football fortunes. However, his thoughts were never far from South Bend.

Lou Holtz was a successful head coach at three college programs before he arrived in Minneapolis. He also did a short stint in the NFL with the New York Jets in 1976. That tumultuous year convinced Holtz that he was not put on this earth to coach professional athletes. Holtz was familiar with the Big Ten, and Michigan since he was an assistant for Woody Hayes at Ohio State in 1968. The fact of the matter was that Lou Holtz could coach. The only question was "would he be around long enough to finish the job?"

As it turned out, Lou Holtz only spent two seasons at Minnesota. He did improve Minnesota's record in the two years he spent in Minneapolis. The Gophers finished the 1985 regular season with a record of 6 wins and 5 losses. However, Notre Dame came calling and Holtz didn't stick around for the bowl game. I don't know for sure, but I'll bet you that Lou Holtz did not buy a home in Minneapolis in 1984. I'm thinking that he rented a home in anticipation of a quick departure at some point in his Gopher future.

Michigan and Minnesota Program Summaries 1979-1983

Coach	Games*	Won-Lost-Tied	Win %	B10 Games	W-L-T	Win %
Bo	24	16-7-1	.688	17	11-5-1	.676
Holtz	22	10-12-0	.456	17	7-10	.412

*Note – These numbers include all of Michigan's bowl games from 1984 to 1985

Once again, Bo out-performed Lou Holtz, just like he did all the other men he coached against at Minnesota. However, his overall record was not as dominant as it had been in the past. Lou Holtz's first season in 1984 (4-7-0) also which happened to be Bo's worst season (6-6-0) at Michigan. The Holtz Era was the only period in Schembechler's tenure that he didn't win at least seventy-three percent of his games.

It is hard to predict what kind of success Lou Holtz might have had at Minnesota if he stayed for five or six years. His two years as the Gopher Football coach were not terrible, but they weren't anything to write home about either! Lou Holtz had one losing season and one winning season at Minnesota and then he was gone! Apparently, there were some recruiting violations that Minnesota had to deal with after his departure. The Holtz Era at Minnesota was short, but not sweet for Minnesota Football fans.

Coach Schembechler vs Coach Holtz 1984-1985

Bo increased his Minnesota "win streak" to eight games for the second time in his career with two straight wins over Lou Holtz and his Gophers. As the numbers show, neither game was close. Michigan won both games by at least twenty-four points. So, the domination continued and Bo just loved keeping the Little Brown Jug in Ann Arbor.

Head-to-Head Summary 1984-1985

Games	Won-Lost-Tied	Win %	Scored/Avg.	Allowed/Avg.	+/- Difference
Home	1-0-0	1.000	31/31.0	7/7.0	+24.0
Away	1-0-0	1.000	48/48.0	7/7.0	+41.0
Totals	2-0-0	1.000	79/39.5	14/7.0	+32.5

The Minnesota Gophers continued to be a "non-threat" to Michigan from 1984 to 1985. Lou Holtz was not a "miracle worker." That's for sure. He didn't do any magic against Bo or the other teams in the Big Ten. His teams were just not very good. Minnesota's offense had trouble scoring against Michigan and the defense simply vanished in the two games that Lou Holtz coached against the Wolverines. Although Bo Schembechler's team slipped in 1984, Michigan came back strong in 1985. Minnesota was a little better in 1984 and 1985, but not that much.

Once again, the fine folks in Minneapolis were wondering if the losing was ever going to end. When would the Gophers find a man who could stand up to Bo and the other Big Ten bullies?

Bo Schembechler and John Gutekunst 1986-1989

John Gutekunst came to Minnesota to work for Lou Holtz as a Defensive Coordinator and Defensive Backs coach. He had a long history of successful assistant coaching jobs at Duke and Virginia Tech before he arrived in Minneapolis. Gutekunst had no Big Ten experience before he arrived in 1984. So, there was a lot to learn. After two seasons at Minnesota, Gutekunst had some valuable experience that would serve him well in future job interviews.

When Lou Holtz bolted to Notre Dame, Gutekunst was named interim coach so that he could coach the Gophers in the 1985 Independence Bowl. Coach Gutekunst kept the team together and focused. Minnesota played well enough to post a 20-13 win over Clemson. John Gutekunst's good work as the "interim" coach helped him land the Head Coach's job in early 1986.

John Gutekunst started his first full season at Minnesota with a perfect record of 1 win and 0 losses. He improved the defense in his first two years as an assistant, but now he had to do the same for the offense. Gutekunst knew that he had a big job ahead of him, but he was up for the challenge and eager to make some improvements in the Gopher Football program.

Four straight Gopher coaches failed to compete with Bo Schembechler's Michigan teams. There wasn't much evidence that things would change heading into the 1986 season. John Gutekunst proved he could lead a team in the Independence Bowl, under difficult circumstances. However, now everyone would have a chance to see what he could do over the course of an entire twelve game season. Would Coach "G" be able to turn things around in Minneapolis? Well, Gopher fans were hoping that he was the right guy. They were tired of losing, especially to Bo Schembechler and Michigan!

Michigan and Minnesota Program Summaries 1986-1989

Coach	Total Games*	Won-Lost-Tied	Win %	B10 Games	W-L-T	Win %
Bo	49	38-10-1	.786	32	27-4-1	.859
Gutekunst	45	20-23-2	.467	32	12-18-2	.406

*Note – These numbers include all bowl games played from 1986 to 1989

Once again, the numbers tell us what really happened. John Gutekunst made some improvements in his first two years and won twelve games. The Gophers slipped badly in 1988 with a record of 2 wins, 7 losses and 2 ties. Minnesota came back to post a winning record of 6-5-0 in 1989, but it wasn't enough to get the support he needed. Michigan won almost twice as many games during this period and lost half as much as the Gophers. It was the same old story for Gopher fans. The Wolverines and the Gophers were still in the same league, but at completely different ends of the conference spectrum. Schembechler remained at the top of the conference and was battling for the league title almost every year. Gutekunst was struggling to stay in the top half of the conference standings.

Coach John Gutekunst's best teams finished with records of 6-5-0 in 1987 and 1989. Bo's Wolverines posted eleven wins in 1985 and came back with ten more in 1989. Michigan never lost more than four games from 1986 to 1989. Minnesota never lost less than five during the same period. I am certain that John Gutekunst and his staff worked their tails off at Minnesota. However, hard work doesn't always trump consistency and continuity. Bo had twenty-one years of consistency and continuity that paid off for Michigan. It also made it very difficult for other teams to catch up since they were always trying to establish a new program every four to six years.

Michigan continued to be strong in conference play as they won at a very high rate (.859) and earned three conference championships during this era. Even though he made some improvements at Minnesota, John Gutekunst never gained any ground on Bo Schembechler and Michigan. When the numbers were all in, Bo's Wolverines remained as one of the top teams in the Big Ten Conference. Minnesota continued to struggle during the Schembechler Years and Michigan Nation loved it!

Coach Schembechler vs Coach Gutekunst 1986-1989

Bo Schembechler was on his second eight-game winning streak against Minnesota when the Gophers came to visit in 1986. First year coach John Gutekunst was coaching a dangerous team. Minnesota had a record of 5 wins and 4 losses heading into their battle with the Wolverines. The 1986 game was played at Michigan Stadium and I was excited for my eight-year old son Marty (Author of *"The Story of The Heisman and The Michigan Man"*), who was attending his first Michigan football game. This time, the Wolverines were ranked number two and sporting a perfect record of nine wins and no losses. Unfortunately, Quarterback Ricky Fogge, running back Darrell Thompson, and a talented kicker named Chip Lohmiller, led the Gophers to a stunning three point upset victory (20-17), ouch, that one really hurt!

The 1986 win over Michigan was John Gutekunst's biggest win at Minnesota. The Gophers were thrilled to take the Little Brown Jug back to Minnesota. Michigan made a lot of mistakes in that game and the Minnesota Footballers took advantage of them. It was the last loss that Bo would suffer against the Gophers, but it probably ruined another great shot at a national championship. Bo Schembechler won the last three games against Coach Gutekunst and finished with a record of 3 wins and 1 loss against the Gopher coach.

Here is a look at the numbers that were posted when Bo and John Gutekunst faced off against each other from 1986 to 1989.

Head-to-Head Summary 1986-1989

Games	Won-Lost-Tied	Win %	Scored/Avg.	Allowed/Avg.	+/- Difference
Home	1-1-0	1.000	31/31.0	7/7.0	+24.0
Away	2-0-0	1.000	48/48.0	7/7.0	+41.0
Totals	3-1-0	1.000	79/39.5	14/7.0	+32.5

As it turned out, Coach John Gutekunst survived for two more years after Bo left in 1989. He finished with three winning seasons, two losing seasons and one was even. Obviously, his upset win in 1986 was his greatest victory at Minnesota. John Gutekunst was the first, and only, Minnesota Football Coach to beat Bo Schembechler in the first series game and take home the "Jug."

Coach Schembechler and Minnesota Summary 1969-1989

Coach Schembechler's record against Minnesota was almost hard to believe. However, his overall record during this time period was just as impressive. Bo's accomplishments at Michigan were significantly better than those of the five Gopher coaches that tried to compete with him from 1969 to 1989. Michigan Football was simply better than Minnesota Football in every measurable category during the Schembechler Era. The Gophers did manage to sneak up on him in two games, but did not have a better season than Michigan at any time from 1969 to 1989. Bottom line – Bo made it tough on Gopher Fans for twenty-one long years. I am certain that they were thrilled to see him go!

Michigan and Minnesota Program Summaries 1969-1989

Coach	Total Games*	W-L-T	Win %	B10 Games	W-L-T	Win %
Bo	247	194-48-5	.796	170	143-24-3	.850
Minnesota	231	99-127-5	.439	172	67-101-4	.401

*Note – These numbers include all bowl games that each team played in from 1969 to 1989

The numbers that Bo achieved during his tenure were amazing. He had Michigan at the top of their game many times, but Minnesota just couldn't get back to their winning ways. Coach Schembechler established his program early and then took advantage of the consistency and continuity that comes with a successful coaching run. Minnesota was always playing "catch-up" during the Bo Era. However, none of the five men who coached the Gophers from 1969 to 1989 ever made any progress against Schembechler and his program.

As I mentioned earlier in this chapter, Michigan flirted with quite a few runs at the national championship. Michigan posted twenty winning seasons and one even season during the Bo Era. Minnesota had eight winning seasons, twelve losing seasons and one season was even.

The Wolverines won or shared thirteen conference titles during the Schembechler Era while the Gophers claimed no conference championships from 1969 to 1989. Michigan was ranked at the end of every Schembechler season except 1984. Minnesota did not finish as a ranked team from 1969 to 1989.

Bo vs Minnesota 1969-1989

Bo record against Minnesota was absolutely stellar. Bo won his first and last games against Minnesota and a bunch in the middle too! He held the advantage over every man that Minnesota put up against him from 1969 to 1989. His nineteen wins in twenty-one games against the

Gophers was a very impressive showing. The Little Brown Jug didn't leave Ann Arbor very often in the Bo Era, but when it did, it was always painful for the spoiled Wolverine Fans.

Head-to-Head Summary 1969-1989

Games	W-L-T	Win %	Scored/Avg.	Allowed/Avg.	+/- Difference
Home	9-1-0	.900	370/37.0	92/9.2	+27.8
Away	10-1-0	.909	392/35.6	139/12.6	+23.0
Totals	19-2-0	.905	762/36.3	231/11.0	+25.3

The impressive numbers shown above allowed Coach Schembechler to enjoy two eight-game winning streaks against the Gophers. However, Coach Schembchler never lost back-to-back games to Minnesota from 1969 to 1989. Michigan shut Minnesota out three times during the Bo Era and only had one game (1977) where they failed to score. The bottom line is simple. Bo's team's dominated Minnesota during his Michigan coaching career which is why he won over ninety-percent of his games against the Gophers.

Bo's outstanding body of work against the Golden Gophers increased Michigan's advantage in the overall series. After the 1989 season, the "Little Brown Jug" rivals had played a total of eighty games. Michigan still held a big advantage with fifty-four wins against twenty-three losses and three ties (54-23-3). The Wolverine winning percent rose from sixty-two percent to sixty-nine percent (.690). Bo was the longest tenured coach in the Big Ten Conference when he left Michigan. This provided a level of stability that helped the Wolverines dominate the Minnesota Gophers.

BO IN HIS CLASSIC POSE. A GREAT PICTURE OF A GREAT MAN
BY A GREAT PHOTOGRAPHER — BOB KALMBACH.

CHAPTER FIVE
BO AND OHIO STATE

THE GREATEST RIVALRY in the history of Michigan football, and arguably the greatest rivalry in college football, was really going strong when Bo arrived. Actually, it was going strong for osu, but not so much for Michigan. No one would have imagined that it could get any more intense, but that's exactly what happened. The dynamics of Bo versus Woody, student versus teacher, "The Team Up North" versus "ohio" was football drama at its best. Some of the greatest games in the rich history of the Michigan-osu rivalry were played in the Bo Era. Let's take a closer look at how Coach Schembechler fared against his former coach and mentor, Woody Hayes, and the other buckeye head coaches he faced from 1969 to 1989.

Bo Schembechler and Woody Hayes 1969-1978

Bo's first test against the buckeyes would come against his "football father" as he referred to Woody prior to their impending battle in November 1969. Woody and his buckeyes rolled into Ann Arbor on a twenty-two-game winning streak. They were ranked number one in the nation and were the defending national champions. Some sportswriters claimed they were the greatest college football team ever! Many experts claimed that the only team that stood a chance against the mighty buckeyes was the Minnesota Vikings of the National Football League.

Beating the buckeyes was Bo's stated goal from his first day on the job. He knew Woody better than any coach in the country and he took advantage of this knowledge. He modeled his offense and defense after ohio state's which meant that his team practiced against the buckeyes every day, all season long. Bo made sure that his conditioning program was tougher than ohio states, he made sure that his practices were more intense than the buckeye practices sessions in

Columbus. Bo made sure that his team knew the magnitude of the game that would be played on November 22, 1969.

Going into his first osu game, Bo's twelfth ranked Wolverines had won seven games and lost twice. So, his record was not as good as Bump Elliott's was the year before (Elliott's team was 8-1 going into the osu game). Basically, the success of Bo's first season rode on the outcome of "The Game." Bo knew it, his coaches knew it, his players knew it and every Michigan fan knew that this was the measuring stick by which people would judge the wisdom of Schembechler's hiring.

Bo's underdogs (osu was favored by 17 points) were sky high for this game and it turned out perfectly for the rookie coach and his Michigan Men. Television announcer Bill Fleming's reaction to the upset win over the number one team in the country was this exclamation "There it is! What has to be the upset of the century."

The 1969 season was the one hundredth year of college football so Fleming had a good basis for his statement. Game number sixty-six in the Michigan vs ohio state series was a classic, at least in the annals of Michigan football history. I'm sure that Woody and his buckeye fans had another word for it.

Bo's eighth win as the Michigan Football Coach was the five hundred and seventeenth victory in program history. Many argue that this was the biggest win in Wolverine Football History because it established Bo's program and, more importantly, it re-established Michigan as a team to be reckoned with in the Big Ten Conference and on the national stage. At a dinner in Columbus, many years later, someone asked Woody which team was his greatest team. His answer was his 1969 team and he looked down the table where Bo was sitting and said, "damn you Bo, you'll never win a bigger game." Later Bo would say, "he (Woody) was right. I never won a bigger game." Bo would go on to win one hundred and eighty-six more games at Michigan, but none would ever be remembered like the shocker heard around the college football world in 1969. One more thing, Bo's Wolverines were never, ever, seventeen-point underdogs again!

Bo's euphoria over his first victory didn't last as long as he would have liked. When he suffered his first heart attack in California while preparing for his first Rose Bowl no one knew for sure if Bo could continue to work at the pace he set during that first year at Michigan. Bo's surgery was a success and it wasn't long before he was back on the practice field working hard to prove to everyone that the 1969 season was no fluke. Of course, Bo was getting ready for the

1970 season, but he was really getting ready for another showdown with Woody in columbus on November 21, 1970.

If the "upset of the century" was Bo's most satisfying win, the 1973 tie with the buckeyes was definitely his greatest disappointment. Michigan and osu were both undefeated. The fourth ranked Wolverines saw the top ranked buckeyes jump out to a 10-0 lead that they maintained until halftime. In the second half, the Wolverines, behind Dennis Franklin, came back to score ten points of their own and almost win the game. Unfortunately, Michigan lost Franklin when he broke his collarbone late in the game and Mike Lantry missed two field goals, one by inches and the game ended in a tie. Since osu had gone to the Rose Bowl the year before, everyone thought that Michigan would go since they tied for the championship with the buckeyes.

Unfortunately for Michigan, the Big Ten had changed the "no repeat" rule so it really wasn't clear who would go bowling. Big Ten Commissioner, Wayne Duke, had previously decided to call for a special vote to determine the best team to represent the conference in the Rose Bowl since the conference had lost three straight Rose Bowl games.

The final vote was six to four in favor of sending the buckeyes to Pasadena. Bo went nuts, but when it was all said and done, he simply called it "a disgrace to the Big 10." He called for Commissioner Wayne Duke to come to Ann Arbor to tell the Wolverines they weren't good enough and to tell his back-up quarterback that he couldn't do the job. Of course, Duke never showed up and Bo never forgot it. Apparently, Schembechler never talked to any of the other men who voted for ohio state – ever!

Bo received an official reprimand for his "unsportsmanlike conduct" and Duke put him on "probation" for a year. The only good that came out of the whole mess was that the conference later voted to change their archaic rule that only one team could go to a bowl game. Not quite what Bo wanted, but progress and tons more money for the conference down the road now that five or six teams go to a bowl every year. As Bo would say, "it was a helluva price to pay."

Woody raised the stakes in the rivalry when he took over at ohio state and he was winning more hands than the Wolverine coaches were. When Bo arrived, he matched Woody's hands and raised the ante. Both coaches pushed their teams to incredible heights so that they each had a shot to win "The Game" and the Big Ten Title at the end of the regular season. Here is a closer look at the "body of work" for Bo and Woody from 1969 to 1978:

Michigan and ohio state Program Summaries 1969-1978

Coach	Games*	Won-Lost-Tied	Win %	B10 Games	W-L-T	Win %
Bo	114	96-15-3	.855	78	69-8-1	.891
Woody	111	88-20-3	.806	781	67-10-1	.865

*Note – These numbers include all bowl games that each team played in from 1969 to 1978

Michigan managed to win eight more games overall than ohio state and two more in conference play from 1969 to 1978. The Wolverines had the edge in winning percentage and both teams won eight conference titles during this ten-year period. Of course, both teams posted winning seasons every year during this incredible era. Woody's buckeyes were very good during this era, but Bo's Wolverines were better.

Michigan was rated nationally for every game of the Bo versus Woody series and the buckeyes were rated nine times. The Wolverines were rated in the top five for eight of these contexts while the buckeyes ended the season with one of these high rankings a total of five times. Five of the games saw both teams rated among the top five teams in the nation when they hit the field. Michigan was never rated number one during this time, but ohio state was the top team in the nation when they took the field in 1969, 1973 and 1975. Of course, Michigan did not win any national championships during this era and neither did the buckeyes. The reason was simple. Bo and Woody ruined each other's chances to win the national championship on numerous occasions or they would blow it in a bowl game.

Coach Schembechler vs Coach Hayes 1969-1978

With Bo and Woody going at it for the first ten years of Bo's tenure, the series became more competitive than ever. The media dubbed the games between the two coaches as the "Ten Year War." Yes, it was pretty intense. Every game but one (Michigan already clinched the title in 1971) was for the Big Ten championship. The annual showdown became a one game season to see who was the best in the conference.

If you look a little closer at the games that comprised the "Ten Year War" you are struck by the body of work that went into these games. From 1969 to 1978 the Wolverines went into "The

Game" with a combined record of ninety-one victories, five defeats and two tie games (91-5-2). These impressive numbers worked out to a winning rate of almost ninety-four percent (.939)! The buckeyes were not quite as good as the Wolverines, (winning percentage was "only" .896) but still way better than the rest of the conference teams. They posted an outstanding record of eighty-five wins, nine losses and two ties (85-9-2) before the annual showdown with the "team up north."

Here's a closer look at what happened in the ten matchups between two of the greatest, and most intense, coaches in college football history (Note- N/R = Not Ranked):

The Ten-Year War Summary

Year	Game Site	Rankings	Winner	Score	BIG Champ	Attendance
1969	Ann Arbor	M#12/osu#2	UM	24-12	UM/osu	103,538*
1970	columbus	M#4/osu#5	osu	9-20	osu	87,331
1971	Ann Arbor	M#3/osu-N/R	UM	10-7	<u>UM</u>	104,016*
1972	columbus	M#3/osu#9	osu	11-14	osu	87,040
1973	Ann Arbor	M#4/osu#1	Tie	10-10	UM/osu	105,223
1974	columbus	M#3/osu#4	osu	10-12	UM/osu	88,243
1975	Ann Arbor	M#4/osu#1	osu	14-21	osu	105,543
1976	columbus	M#4/osu#8	UM	22-0	UM/osu	88,250
1977	Ann Arbor	M#5/osu#4	UM	14-6	UM/osu	106,024
1978	columbus	M#6/osu#16	UM	14-3	UM/MSU	88.358

*NCAA record crowd at the time

Every game between Bo's Wolverines and Woody's buckeyes was super intense, which is why they called this classic series the "Ten Year War." The average margin of victory between these two bitter foes was about eight points (7.9) per game. There was only one shutout – the Wolverine's whitewashing (22-0) of the buckeyes in 1976 at the horseshoe - oh how sweet it was.

The winning team only managed to score twenty or more points in four of the ten games and twenty-four was the highest number of points scored in the "War Years." Michigan averaged about thirteen points (13.8) in these extra intense games while the buckeyes averaged just over ten points (10.5) per contest. When Bo's Wolverines won in 1978, for the third straight year, it was hard to imagine that the "war" was over. That's how it worked out after the 1979 Gator Bowl when Woody was fired for striking a player from Clemson at the end of another disappointing bowl loss.

For the record, Bo finished the "Ten Year War" series with five wins, four losses and the one, unforgettable, tie. Bo and Woody tied for the number of conference championships during this period. Woody's buckeyes won two conference championships during the "Ten Year War" and shared six more with Bo and his Wolverines for a total of eight trophies. Bo's footballers won one conference championship along with the seven he shared with osu for a total of eight. The only other conference team to get their name on the conference trophy during this era was Michigan State who tied with the Wolverines in 1978.

Head-to-Head Summary 1969-1978

Games	Won-Lost-Tied	Win %	Scored/Avg.	Allowed/Avg.	+/- Difference
Home	3-1-1	.700	72/14.4	56/11.2	+3.2
Away	2-3-0	.400	66/13.2	49/9.8	+3.4
Totals	5-4-1	.550	138/13.8	105/10.5	+3.3

Yes, it was an amazing ten years that went beyond normal football rivalries. Both coaches were bigger than life and their personal rivalry added an incredible edge to an already intense series. Bo held a slight advantage over Woody's teams, but dominated everyone else in the conference. They won sixty-four out of sixty-eight conference games which was ninety-four percent of their games (.941). Only three other conference teams were able to beat the Wolverines during this Era (MSU, Minnesota and Purdue). Woody's teams were outstanding as well in conference play. They won sixty-three of sixty-eight games for a winning rate of almost ninety-three percent (.926). It was an amazing run for both coaches and both programs. Michigan and ohio state would continue to be in the hunt for the conference championship most of the time, but the conference would no longer be the Big Two and the Little Eight. After Woody's firing, the Michigan vs ohio state series would continue to be hard fought, but it would never, ever, be the same!

Bo Schembechler and Earle Bruce 1979-1987

Woody was replaced by Earle Bruce who would become the only Big Ten coach to have a winning record against Bo. Bruce earned instant credibility with the ohio state faithful when his buckeyes snapped Michigan's three game winning streak with a three-point victory (18-15) in 1979. Neither Bo nor Earle Bruce could put together more than a two-game winning streak in the series during the next nine years.

Michigan and ohio state continued to play some very good football during the Schembechler vs Bruce Era, but it was not as ridiculous as the "War years." Neither team was as dominant from 1979 to 1987 as they were from 1969 to 1978. In fact, the numbers clearly show that Earl Bruce and his buckeyes had the edge over Bo and his Wolverines. Take a look at the numbers below and see what I mean.

Michigan and ohio state Program Summaries 1979-1987

Coach	Games*	Won-Lost-Tied	Win %	B10 Games	W-L-T	Win %
Bo	109	79-29-1	.729	76	59-16-1	.783
Bruce	108	81-26-1	.754	74	57-17-0	.770

*Note – These numbers include all bowl games that each team played in from 1979 to 1987

Bo would tell you that Earle Bruce was a damn good football coach and the numbers would verify such a claim. Earle Bruce posted a better overall record than Bo did from 1979 to 1987. He managed to win two more games during this period and posted a slightly higher winning percentage. Bo had the edge in Big Ten play by the same margin of two games and did post a better winning percentage, but not by much. Earle Bruce led his teams to four conference titles during this era while Bo claimed three Big Ten Championships. Again, the days of the Big Two and the Little Eight were gone, but the buckeyes had the edge on Bo and his Wolverines.

Both teams posted winning regular season records during this period. However, with the exception of 1979, when the buckeyes were rated number two in the nation, they were usually fighting it out for some respect at the conference level, but not nationally. Michigan was rated seven times during this era and ohio state was rated six times. The buckeyes were rated in the top five twice (1979 and 1980), but the Wolverines were never ranked higher than sixth when the two teams faced off in their season finale. Of course, none of "The Games" in this period were top five matchups as in the "War Years." The final indicator that both teams had slipped a little was in 1987 when Michigan and ohio state were both unranked when lame duck coach Earle Bruce led his buckeyes to a big upset in the Big House.

Coach Schembechler vs Coach Bruce 1979-1987

Again, the rivalry continued to be the most competitive game in the conference every year, but it wasn't the same without Woody. I doubt if Bo let up much in his preparations, or his record against Earl Bruce would have been worse. Both teams continued to be very good, but were not able to sustain the Big Two and Little Eight tradition that started with Bo and Woody. Here's what happened in the nine matchups between Bo and Earle Bruce. I call them the "Nine Year Battles." (Note- N/R = Not Ranked):

The Nine-Year Battles Summary

Year	Game Site	Rankings	Winner	Score	BIG Champ	Attendance
1979	Ann Arbor	M#14/osu#2	osu	15-18	osu	106,255*
1980	columbus	M#10/osu#5	UM	9-3	UM	88,827
1981	Ann Arbor	M#7/osu-N/R	osu	9-14	osu/Iowa	106,043
1982	columbus	M#13/osuN/R	osu	14-24	UM	90,252
1983	Ann Arbor	M#8/osu#10	UM	24-14	Illinois	106,115
1984	columbus	MN/R/osu#11	osu	6-21	osu	90,286
1985	Ann Arbor	M#6/osu#12	UM	27-17	Iowa	106,102
1986	columbus	M#6/osu#7	UM	26-24	UM/osu	90,674
1987	Ann Arbor	M-N/R/osuN/R	osu	20-23	MSU	106,031

*NCAA record crowd at the time

In the final analysis, all of the games between Bo and Earle Bruce were as hard-fought and competitive as any in the long history of the series. Bo won four games and lost five games to Bruce and his buckeyes. Again, Earle Bruce was a good football coach who earned Bo's respect, but not that of the unforgiving buckeye fans and the university president. Bruce was fired at the end of the 1987 football season. Athletic Director Rick Bay, a Michigan Man, resigned as a result of the way the buckeye administration handled the whole affair.

Head-to-Head Summary 1979-1987

Games	Won-Lost-Tied	Win %	Scored/Avg.	Allowed/Avg.	+/- Difference
Home	2-3-0	.400	95/19.0	93/18.6	+0.40
Away	2-2-0	.500	55/13.8	72/18.0	-4.2
Totals	4-5-0	.444	150/16.7	165/18.3	-1.6

The games were just a little closer as the average margin of victory dropped to about six points (6.3). The defenses weren't quite as strong as the average number of points scored in the contests went up. Michigan averaged about seventeen points (16.6) during this phase of the series, up slightly from about fourteen points (13.8) per game average versus Woody.

The buckeyes averaged just over eighteen points (18.3) per game behind the offensive minded Bruce. This increase of almost eight points (7.8) per game must have pained Bo greatly as well as his negative point differential against the buckeyes. The Earle Bruce "haters" got their way when he was fired in 1987. Apparently, he had some gambling transgressions that he couldn't overcome so it was time to put another man on the sidelines. However, buckeye fans would learn that it would be hard to beat the numbers that Earle Bruce posted against Bo Schembechler and Michigan.

Bo Schembechler and John Cooper – 1988 to 1989

Bo's last two games against osu were against Bruce's replacement, John Cooper. Cooper's Arizona State team defeated Schembechler's Wolverines in the 1986 Rose Bowl game, which is one of the reasons he got the osu job. Cooper knew what he was getting into when he came to Columbus, but he must have figured he could handle it. Let's see how he did during the first two years of his tenure compared to the man named Schembechler at the school "Up North."

Michigan and ohio state Program Summaries 1969-1978

Coach	Games*	Won-Lost-Tied	Win %	B10 Games	W-L-T	Win %
Bo	24	19-4-1	.813	16	15-0-1	.969
Cooper	23	12-10-1	.543	16	8-7-1	.531

*Note – These numbers include all bowl games that each team played in from 1988 to 1989

Bo fared much better against Cooper's buckeyes than he did against his Sun Devil team as the Wolverines won two games out of two games. Bo finished strong and must have made things very difficult for John Cooper. The programs appeared to be heading in completely different directions. Bo's numbers were reminiscent of the "War Years," but Cooper's looked more like the Great Depression as far as buckeye fans were concerned. Bo had the edge in every category and won two Big Ten Titles to boot while ohio state won zero. It is amazing that John Cooper didn't get fired, but he was smart enough to get a long-term contract when he signed on with ohio state. So, he survived.

Michigan was much better than the buckeyes during this era, period! Michigan was not in the hunt for any national titles when they faced off against the buckeyes in 1988. However, Michigan was rated in both contests against Cooper and the buckeyes were ranked once. Although they were ranked number three when they defeated the buckeyes in 1989, a national title for Bo just wasn't meant to be.

Coach Schembechler vs Coach Cooper 1988 to 1989

The head to head match ups between Schembechler and Cooper were unlike any in the previous nineteen years. They were free-wheeling, high scoring affairs that didn't look anything like the "War Years" or most of the games between Earl Bruce and Bo Schembechler. The numbers that the two teams put on the board in the two games between Cooper and Schembechler would have taken five years to achieve in the previous eras.

Head-to-Head Summary 1988-1989

Games	Won-Lost-Tied	Win %	Scored/Avg.	Allowed/Avg.	+/- Difference
Home	1-0-0	1.000	28/28.0	18/18.0	+18.0
Away	1-0-0	1.000	34/34.0	31/31.0	+3.0
Totals	2-0-0	1.000	62/31.0	49/24.5	+6.5

Bo saved the best for last in his buckeye rivalry. You can't do better than two wins in two games. He was probably happy with the offensive numbers his teams posted in these two games, but probably not the defensive statistics. Again, he probably made things real tough on John Cooper, but that's the way it was and continues to be in the greatest rivalry in college football.

Bo Schembechler and ohio state 1969-1989

Bo's impact on the Michigan Football Program was significant and long-lasting. His twenty-one years of coaching produced some exceptional numbers and helped Michigan to rise to national power once again. Let's take a final look to see how his work compared to that of his greatest rival, the school down south called ohio state.

Michigan and ohio state Program Summaries 1969-1989

Coach	Games*	Won-Lost-Tied	Win %	B10 Games	W-L-T	Win %
Bo	247	194-48-5	.796	170	143-24-3	.850
osu	242	181-56-5	.758	168	132-34-2	.791

*Note – These numbers include all bowl games that each team played in from 1969 to 1989

The numbers verify that Bo did extremely well during his twenty-one-year tenure at Michigan. He held the edge over the buckeyes in every important area during this period, but not by much. The buckeyes were a football powerhouse during the Bo Era, but Michigan was better. Bo knew that he had to push his coaches and players to incredible heights to compete with Woody and the rest of the buckeye coaches that he faced during his tenure. Thank goodness, Schembechler's beloved players were willing to pay the price!

Michigan flirted with runs at the national championship and so did the buckeyes, but they usually beat each other when the chips were on the line, got ambushed by one of the "Little Eight" or lost a big bowl game so that did not work out for either coach. Michigan had a winning regular season in all twenty-one years of the Schembechler Era and finished as a nationally ranked team in twenty of Bo's twenty-one years. The buckeyes managed to post twenty winning seasons during this era and finished with a total seventeen end of season rankings in the Associated Press football poll. The Wolverines won or shared thirteen conference titles during the Schembechler Era while the buckeyes claimed twelve championships.

Coach Schembechler vs ohio state 1969-1989

The bottom line was that Bo finished strong against the buckeyes and he was able to finish with a winning record (11-9-1) against Michigan's greatest rival. It took an unbelievable amount of hard work and determination to earn a two-win edge over the buckeyes, but he did it.

Head-to-Head Summary 1969-1989

Games	Won-Lost-Tied	Win %	Scored/Avg.	Allowed/Avg.	+/- Difference
Home	6-4-1	.591	195/17.7	167/15.2	+2.5
Away	5-5-0	.500	155/15.5	152/15.2	+0.3
Totals	**11-9-1**	**.548**	**350/16.7**	**319/15.2**	**+1.5**

The numbers displayed on the "Head-to-Head" charts show how close the competition between Bo and the buckeyes was. The points were very hard to come by and so were the wins. It was an intensely close series against two superb football programs. The fact that Coach Schembechler finished with a two-win advantage and a positive point differential of just over one point per game (+1.5) says it all about Michigan and ohio state. It all added up to some of the best on-the-field drama in college football history.

As of November 1989, the Michigan-ohio state rivalry was firmly established as one of the greatest, if not the greatest, rivalry in college football. Michigan improved greatly against everyone else and held the edge against the buckeyes from 1969 to 1989. At end of the Bo Era, a total of eighty-six games had been played in the series. Michigan still held the advantage with forty-seven wins to their credit while osu owned thirty-four victories and five ties were also in the books (48-33-5). Michigan's winning rate actually decreased from sixty percent overall to just over fifty-eight percent (.587). Bo had met Woody and his successors "head on" in twenty-one monumental games. Coach Schembechler made sure that the Wolverines were focused on the team from ohio and he elevated Michigan's performance against the buckeyes and everyone else in the conference.

CHAPTER SIX

BO AND MICHIGAN STATE

ONCE AGAIN, BO made it very clear when he arrived in Ann Arbor that his number one job was to beat state – ohio state. He didn't talk much about Michigan State when he started coaching the Maize and Blue. Duffy Daughtery and his Spartans didn't even seem to be on the radar screen when Bo arrived in Ann Arbor. However, it was clear to everyone in Wolverine Nation that the Spartans had become the dominant team in the State of Michigan and this had to change. During his twenty-one-year tenure Bo would face off against four/five different Spartan coaches. Let's see how well Coach Schembechler's efforts compared to those of the Spartan football leaders from 1969 to 1989.

Bo Schembechler and Duffy Daughtery 1969-1972

Duffy Daughterty and his Spartans had the best college football program in the State of Michigan in 1969 although Bo didn't seem to care. His job was to beat ohio state, win the conference title and go to the Rose Bowl. Michigan State was clearly the better team in the State of Michigan when Bo took the reins in Ann Arbor. He didn't seem to get the "state" part of the "in state" rivalry with the team in East Lansing. That all changed on October 18, 1969 when Bo took his thirteenth ranked Wolverines to Spartan Stadium for his first encounter with Duffy Daugherty's unranked footballers.

The Wolverines lost by ten points (23-13) and it gave Bo something to think about on the bus ride home. In the staff meeting following Bo's first conference road loss, he declared "we are now here to beat two teams." The Spartans were now on Coach Schembechler's radar and they would remain there for the next twenty years! After his initial "wake up call" Bo kept Duffy and his Spartans on his radar and won the next three games and a lot more against everyone else. Although Bo always seemed to be preparing for Woody and ohio state, he did enough to prep for Duffy and his Spartans. In four short years, Bo's Wolverines were becoming the best team in the State of Michigan and one of the best in the country. Take a look at the numbers below and see how both men compared.

<u>Michigan and Michigan State Program Summaries 1969-1972</u>

Coach	Games*	Won-Lost-Tied	Win %	B10 Games	W-L-T	Win %
Bo	44	38-6-0	.864	30	27-3-0	.900
Duffy	42	19-22-1	.464	30	15-14-1	.517

*Note – These numbers include all bowl games that each team played in from 1969 to 1972

Bo had the edge over Duffy and his Spartans in every category from 1969 to 1972. He doubled the Spartans overall victory total and did much better in conference play. Michigan posted four winning seasons in the Bo versus Duffy Era, but the Spartans only posted one. Both teams from the great State of Michigan were still in the same league (The Big Ten), but the Wolverines were now at a different level.

Bo held the advantage in Big Ten play by almost three wins per season. He also led his team to three conference titles in four years while Duffy's Spartans won none. Coach Schembechler's teams were now part of the Big Ten's "Big Two" while the Spartans had slipped to the middle of the "Little Eight."

Coach Schembechler vs Coach Daughtery 1969-1972

Bo was a quick study and he could connect the dots faster than a lot of other coaches. After his shaky start against Duffy's Spartans Bo figured things out pretty quickly. He defeated the Spartans in the next three contests and the games weren't that close. Take a look at the numbers below to see what happened in the four matchups between Bo Schembechler and Duffy Daughtery.

Head-to-Head Summary 1969-1972

Games	Won-Lost-Tied	Win %	Scored/Avg.	Allowed/Avg.	+/- Difference
Home	2-0-0	1.000	44/22.0	20/10.0	+12.0
Away	1-1-0	.500	36/18.0	36/18.0	Even
Totals	**3-1-0**	**.750**	**80/20.0**	**56/14.0**	**+6.0**

Another indicator that things were going in the right direction for Michigan and the wrong direction for the Spartans was the national rankings. Michigan was ranked nationally four times in four games (twice in the top five) when they played the Spartans, but Duffy's teams were unranked for every game. The numbers now favored the Wolverines across the board and football was starting to get ugly again in East Lansing. Anyone who knew anything about college football figured it was time for a change in the Spartan Football program.

Duffy Daughtery had a very good run while he was at Michigan State, but Bo's arrival was the beginning of the end for the Smiling Spartan coach with the quick wit and the twinkle in his eye. Coach Daughtery was out of quips and smiles after the 1972 season. Spartan fans weren't smiling either as the hated Wolverines were back on top in the State of Michigan. Michigan had gained a lot of ground in four short years and there was no end in sight. Schembechler was putting together a power house football program that was starting to put Michigan State in the rear-view mirror.

Bo Schembechler and Denny Stolz 1973-1975

Michigan State hired a young, energetic man named Denny Stolz to replace the legendary Daughtery, but it didn't work out too well for Stolz or the Spartans. Stolz probably had marching orders that charged him to beat Schembechler and the Wolverines or else! Unfortunately for Stolz and Michigan State, it turned out to be "or else." Denny Stolz made some improvements in the Spartan Football program, but they weren't good enough. He also failed to beat Schembechler so that didn't help his cause or his job security. Here is a look at how the two coaches and programs compared from 1973 to 1975.

Michigan and Michigan State Program Summaries 1973-1975

Coach	Games*	Won-Lost-Tied	Win %	B10 Games	W-L-T	Win %
Bo	34	28-3-3	.868	24	21-2-1	.896
Stolz	332	19-13-1	.591	24	14-9-1	.604

*Note – These numbers include all bowl games that each team played in from 1973 to 1975

Again, Bo had the edge over Denny Stolz and his Spartans in every category from 1973 to 1975. Bo's Wolverines posted nine more wins overall and had seven more in conference play in three years. Michigan had three very winning seasons in three years while the Spartans posted two. Again, Stolz made some improvements, but they fell short of expectations.

Bo continued to have the advantage in Big Ten play by almost three wins per season. Michigan won two conference titles during this period while Michigan State won zero. The Wolverines were still at the elite level in conference play while the Spartans were stuck in the middle of the pack. Even though Denny Stolz was doing a lot of things right at Michigan State, he could not close the gap between his team and the Wolverines. Bo Schembechler was making it hard to be the second-best football team in the State of Michigan.

Coach Schembechler vs Coach Stolz 1973-1975

Bo wasn't losing too many games to anybody except ohio state at this point in his career so Denny Stolz was no exception. Schembechler's Wolverines dominated the Spartans during the tenure of Denny Stolz. It started with a shutout in East Lansing (31-0), a fourteen-point defeat in Ann Arbor (21-7) and finished with a ten-point loss (16-6) in Spartan Stadium. The numbers told a sad Spartan story here, but Wolverine Nation loved it!

Head-to-Head Summary 1973-1975

Games	Won-Lost-Tied	Win %	Scored/Avg.	Allowed/Avg.	+/- Difference
Home	1-0-0	1.000	21/21.0/22.0	7/7.0	+14.0
Away	2-0-0	1.000	47/23.5	6/3.0	+20.5
Totals	**3-0-0**	**1.000**	**68/22.7**	**13/4.3**	**+18.4**

Denny Stolz made some solid improvements in the Spartan Football Program, but you couldn't tell by his performance against Schembechler's Wolverines. Again, Michigan was ranked nationally in all three Spartan matchups (twice in the top five) while Denny's teams were only ranked once. The numbers favored the Wolverines in every measurable category. Spartan fans continued not to be happy with Michigan State Football. Denny Stolz loved the Green and White, but the love was not returned. At the end of the 1975 season Denny Stolz was gone. Where would the Spartans find the man who could stop Schembechler and the "Arrogant Asses" from Ann Arbor?

Bo Schembechler and Darryl Rogers 1976-1979

While Denny Stolz seemed like a pretty nice guy, Darryl Rogers seemed to have an "edge" about him especially when it came to the Michigan Wolverines. He was on a mission to beat Michigan and Bo Schembechler, that's for sure. Let's see how things worked out for the new Spartan Football Leader and his program from 1976 to 1979.

Michigan and Michigan State Program Summaries 1976-1979

Coach	Games*	Won-Lost-Tied	Win %	B10 Games	W-L-T	Win %
Bo	48	38-10-0	.792	32	27-5-0	.844
Rogers	44	24-18-2	.568	32	19-12-1	.609

*Note – These numbers include all bowl games that each team played in from 1976 to 1979

Once again, Bo steamrolled another coach that the Spartans put in his way. Schembechler's teams continued to be much better than Roger's teams from 1976 to 1979. Michigan won fourteen more games in this four-year span and posted a winning rate that was over two hundred percentage points better than the Spartans. The Wolverines continued to rack up winning seasons every year while the Spartans only had two winning records during this four-year period. Darryl Rogers actually won at a slightly lesser rate than Denny Stolz overall but he was a little bit better in conference play. Regardless, his efforts were not good enough and he left the Spartans to coach at Arizona State. Who would be the Spartans turn to now to get this thing around?

Schembechler's Wolverines continued to have the advantage in Big Ten play but it was only by an average of two wins per season with Rogers at the helm. Michigan shared three conference titles during this period, two with ohio state and one with the Spartans in 1978. The Wolverines were still at the elite level in conference play while the Spartans were just trying to get better.

Coach Schembechler vs Coach Rogers 1976-1979

Bo won his first two against Darryl Rogers making it nine wins in a row after losing the first game to Duffy in 1969. However, Rogers put together his best team in 1978 and went to Ann Arbor to play the "Arrogant Asses." Rogers left with a huge upset victory (24-15) over fifth ranked Michigan in what was probably the most satisfying win of his Spartan career.

Bo defeated Rogers and his Spartans in East Lansing the last time they faced each other by fourteen points (21-7) and another Michigan State coach moved on. Here is a look at what happened when Bo Schembechler and Darryl Rogers teams faced off against each other from 1976 to 1979.

Head-to-Head Summary 1976-1979

Games	Won-Lost-Tied	Win %	Scored/Avg.	Allowed/Avg.	+/- Difference
Home	1-1-0	.500	57/28.5	34/17.0	+11.5
Away	2-0-0	1.000	45/22.5	21/10.5	+12.0
Totals	3-1-0	.750	102/25.5	55/13.8	+11.7

Darryl Rogers learned the hard way that beating Bo and his Michigan teams was easier said than done. Name calling didn't really help although he tried his best. The key to beating Bo's teams was a strong defense and a consistent offense that could points on the board without committing a lot of turnovers. The Spartans were not able to do that in most of their games against Bo's Wolverines.

Like Denny Stolz before him, Darryl Rogers was winning more football games than he was losing, but Bo was beating just about everybody he played except the buckeyes. A record of one win and three losses in four games against Michigan was not good enough. Darryl Rogers didn't think it was going to get any better so, he jumped at the chance to coach Arizona State.

Schembechler's Wolverines were simply playing at a different level and everybody in the State of Michigan knew which team was the best. Michigan was ranked nationally in all four games (three were in the top five) against Rogers and his Spartans while Michigan State was ranked just once. The numbers continued to favor the Wolverines in every measurable category, and one win over Michigan every four years probably wasn't going to cut it. Rogers decided to go while he could and left the very difficult tasks of beating Bo Schembechler and Michigan to someone else.

Bo Schembechler and Muddy Waters 1980-1982

For Michigan State, "Someone Else" became a man named Frank "Muddy" Waters. Muddy Waters played fullback for the Spartans from 1946 to 1949. He became a coaching legend at Hillsdale College winning almost seventy-four percent (.739) of his games from 1954 to 1974. He was in the fifth year of building a successful program at Saginaw Valley State College when the Spartans came calling for his coaching expertise.

Muddy Waters new job at Michigan State was simple, just not easy. The simple part was that he only had to do two things: 1) build a winning Big Ten program and 2) start beating Schembechler. The "not easy" part was doing it. Muddy Waters played in the Big Ten and coached at a high level at the small college level. Could he take his successful experiences to the highest level of college football and actually compete against Schembechler and his Wolverines?

Michigan and Michigan State Program Summaries 1980-1982

Coach	Games*	Won-Lost-Tied	Win %	B10 Games	W-L-T	Win %
Bo	36	27-9-0	.750	26	22-4-0	.846
Waters	33	10-23-0	.303	26	8-18-0	.308

*Note – These numbers include all of Michigan's bowl games from 1980 to 1982

Well as it turned out, Muddy had no magic at Michigan State. His teams were pretty awful and that's the truth. The Spartan program went backwards from 1980 to 1982. Denny Stolz and

Darryl had three things in common after their short coaching tenures at Michigan State. First, they both had losing records against Bo and Michigan. Second, they both had winning records overall. Third, they both had winning records in the Big Ten during their time in East Lansing.

In the end, the only thing that Muddy Waters would have in common with Denny and Darryl was that he too had a losing record against Schembechler. Unfortunately, for him and Spartan Nation, Waters did not have a winning record overall, or in Big Ten play. Muddy Waters had three straight losing seasons and never won more than five games in three very long seasons. Meanwhile, Bo's Wolverines posted winning records in three years and also won two Big Ten titles. Overall, it was a tough three years for Spartan Football fans and Muddy Waters was looking for a new job.

Coach Schembechler vs Coach Waters 1980-1982

Bo won all three games against Muddy Waters and only the first one was close (27-23). Bo's record versus the Spartans improved to twelve wins and only two losses. His Spartan winning streak was up to four and the Wolverines were on another roll. The numbers below tell another happy Wolverine Story from 1980 to 1982.

Head-to-Head Summary 1980-1982

Games	Won-Lost-Tied	Win %	Scored/Avg.	Allowed/Avg.	+/- Difference
Home	2-0-0	1.000	58/29.0	40/20.0	+9.0
Away	1-0-0	1.000	38/38.0	20/20.0	+18.0
Totals	3-0-0	1.000	96/32.0	60/20.0	+12.0

Muddy Waters and his teams were simply not a factor for Michigan while he was coaching the Spartans. His teams were not very good. Although they were able to score an average of twenty points against Bo's defenses, his defenses allowed way too many points which is why he was winless against Coach Schembechler and his Wolverines.

Although Bo Schembechler's teams slipped a little bit in the early 1980s, they were still much better than the Spartans and clearly the best team in the state. Michigan was only ranked once when they played the Spartans, but Michigan State entered every game as a non-ranked team. The numbers continued to favor the Wolverines in every measurable category, and frustrated Spartans were wondering if the losing was ever going to end. Was there anyone who could stand up to Bo and his Wolverines?

Bo Schembechler and George Perles 1983-1989

Four straight Spartan coaches had failed to compete with Bo Schembechler's Michigan teams. Would the losing ever end? Would Michigan State ever put together another winning tradition? Would they ever get to the Rose Bowl again? These were the questions that Spartan fans were asking and they wanted answers and better results.

Michigan State turned to another former Spartan who also had a very impressive coaching resume. He served as a Defensive Line coach at Michigan State from 1959 to 1970 and then moved on to the National Football League. He helped build the famed "Steel Curtain" defense in Pittsburgh and worked his way up from Defensive Line coach to Defensive Coordinator and then to Assistant Head Coach. Oh, by the way, he also earned four Super Bowl Rings along the way.

George Perles was a winner! He was determined to re-build the Spartan football program into a power house that would make things difficult for Bo Schembechler and the rest of Wolverine Nation. Here is a closer look at how the work of these two men compared from 1983 to 1989.

Michigan and Michigan State Program Summaries 1983-1989

Coach	Total Games*	Won-Lost-Tied	Win %	B10 Games	W-L-T	Win %
Bo	86	63-20-2	.753	58	46-10-2	.810
Perles	82	46-33-3	.579	58	35-20-3	.629

*Note – These numbers include all bowl games played from 1983 to 1989

George Perles certainly made Spartan Fans forget Muddy Waters although not in the first year. He only won four games, lost six and tied one in 1983. Meanwhile Bo's Michigan team finished at nine wins and three losses. Year two was a little better for Perles as he posted a winning record in the Big Ten, went to a bowl game and finished even at six wins and six losses. As it turned out, this was the same record that the Wolverines finished with in 1984.

Coach Perles was putting his program in place and he posted five straight winning seasons, just like Bo, from 1985 to 1989. So, the Spartans were getting better, but the Wolverines were still the best team in the State of Michigan. Bo won more games overall, won more conference games and had much higher winning rates.

Michigan continued to be strong in conference play as they won at a very high rate (.810) and earned three conference championships during this era. George Perles was gaining ground on Bo and his Wolverines. He earned Michigan State's first conference championship since 1978 when his Spartans went undefeated in conference play (7-0-1) in 1987. They also won the 1988 Rose Bowl.

When the numbers were all in, Bo's Wolverines were still the best team in the State of Michigan and the best team from Michigan in the Big Ten Conference. They continued their great play during Coach Schembechler's tenure that finally ended in 1989.

Coach Schembechler vs Coach Perles 1983-1989

Bo defeated George Perles in their first matchup in East Lansing in 1983. Schembechler's fifth straight victory over MSU stretched his Spartan winning streak to five games and increased his record to thirteen wins in fifteen games. George Perles turned the tables in 1984 as his hungry Spartans defeated Bo's Wolverines by twelve points (19-7) in Ann Arbor. This was the game that saw Jim Harbaugh suffer a broken shoulder and it was a pivotal loss in what turned out to be Bo's worst season at Michigan.

Here is a look at the numbers that were posted when Michigan and Michigan State faced off against each other in the Great State of Michigan from 1983 to 1989.

Head-to-Head Summary 1983-1989

Games	Won-Lost-Tied	Win %	Scored/Avg.	Allowed/Avg.	+/- Difference
Home	2-1-0	.667	51/17.0	28/9.3	+7.7
Away	3-1-0	.750	94/23.5	24/6.0	+17.5
Totals	5-2-0	.714	145/20.7	52/7.4	+13.3

As it turned out, Bo and George became good friends, just not when they were coaching against each other. They shared a mutual respect that continued long after Bo left coaching. George Perles was a very good football coach and he did things the right way. He re-established the Michigan State Football program and made the Spartans more competitive in the Big Ten Conference. He came out on the short end of most of his encounters with Bo's Wolverines, but became the first and only Spartan Coach to win two games against Coach Schembechler.

Coach Schembechler and Michigan State – Overall 1969-1989

Once again, Bo's impact on the Michigan Football Program was significant and long-lasting. His twenty-one years of coaching produced some exceptional numbers and helped Michigan rise to national power and Big Ten dominance once again. Let's take a final look to see how his work compared to that of his in-state rival, the Michigan State Spartans.

Coach	Total Games*	W-L-T	Win %	B10 Games	W-L-T	Win %
Bo	247	194-48-5	.796	170	143-24-3	.850
MSU	234	118-109-7	.519	170	91-73-6	.553

*Note – These numbers include all bowl games that each team played in from 1969 to 1989

Much to the chagrin of Spartans fans everywhere, Bo's accomplishments at Michigan were significantly better than those of the five Spartans he coached against from 1969 to 1989. Michigan Football was simply better than Michigan State Football in every measurable category. The Spartans managed to have a few good years during the Schembechler Era, but Bo had twenty of them along with five or six great seasons. The distance between the two programs was way more than the forty-five miles from Ann Arbor to East Lansing and everybody in the Mitten State knew it. Bo made it tough on Spartan Fans and they were thrilled to see him go.

As I mentioned earlier in this chapter, Michigan flirted with runs at the national championship, but not the Spartans. Their national championship runs were now just a faded memory. Michigan had a winning regular season in all twenty-one years of the Schembechler Era and finished as a nationally ranked team in twenty of Bo's twenty-one years. The Spartans managed to post ten winning seasons during this era and only finished in the final rankings four times. The Wolverines won or shared thirteen conference titles during the Schembechler Era while the Spartans claimed two championships.

Coach Schembechler vs Michigan State 1969-1989

After losing his first Spartan game in 1969, Bo really turned things around with the in-state rivals. Bo's final record against the Spartans finished at seventeen victories, four defeats and no ties (17-4-0) – nobody in Michigan Football history achieved that many wins against the Spartans. He posted a winning record against all five men he coached against on the Michigan State sideline. Only three of the five men managed to beat him and only George Perles beat him twice.

Head-to-Head Summary 1969-1989

Games	W-L-T	Win %	Scored/Avg.	Allowed/Avg.	+/- Difference
Home	8-2-0	.800	231/23.1	129/12.9	+10.2
Away	9-2-0	.818	260/23.6	107/9.7	+13.9
Totals	17-4-0	.810	491/23.4	236/11.2	+12.2

Bo's success against the Spartans also gave Michigan the edge in the Paul Bunyon Trophy series with twenty-one wins, fourteen wins and two ties (21-14-4). Bo never lost back-to-back games to Michigan State, but had four winning streaks against the Spartans.

Schlembechler's teams won eight straight games from 1970 to 1977, five straight games from 1979 to 1983, and two straight games twice (1985-1986 and 1988-1989). Bo's defenses shut the Spartans out four different times, but his teams always scored at least seven points against the Spartans.

By the time Bo retired, the advantage in the "in state" series had swung all the way back to Michigan. At the end of the 1989 season, Michigan had dramatically increased their total wins in the overall series. The Wolverines now had fifty-four wins, twenty-three losses and five ties (54-23-5). Bo's winning ways increased Michigan's series winning percentage from sixty-four percent when he started to seventy-one percent when he left. Michigan State was pushing hard to be the best team in the State of Michigan when Duffy Daugherty was running the show in East Lansing. However, the arrival of Bo Shembechler changed everything, but not until 1970.

Bo was the longest tenured coach in the Big Ten Conference when he left Michigan. This provided a level of stability that helped the Wolverines take back the State of Michigan. Bo's teams also regained bragging rights about which program was the best in the Great Lakes State. Schembechler's television show, Michigan Replay, was broadcast throughout the state. He owned the state's high school recruiting territory and, with Don Canham's help, made sure that Ann Arbor was the second largest city in the state on football Saturdays. Yes, Bo turned a lot of things around during his tenure. He personally ensured that Michigan, again, was the best football program in the State of Michigan and one of the best in the country – got it?

Coach Schembechler's Rivals Summary 1969-1989

Rival games are the best ones to win and the hardest ones to lose. Each contest only counts as one victory or one defeat, but those rival wins are a little sweeter and the rival losses are just a lot tougher on the losing team. That's just the way it is. Let's take a final look at the numbers below and see how Coach Schembechler did against Michigan's rivals at home and on the road from 1969 to 1989.

	Home		Away		Overall Record	
Rival	**W-L-T**	**Win %**	**W-L-T**	**Win %**	**W-L-T**	**Win %**
Notre Dame	2-3-0	.400	2-3-0	.400	4-6-0	.400
Minnesota	9-1-0	.900	10-1-0	.909	19-2-0	.904
ohio state	6-4-1	.590	5-5-0	.500	11-9-1	.547
Michigan State	8-2-0	.800	9-2-0	.818	17-4-0	.810
Overall	**25-10-1**	**.708**	**25-12-0**	**.676**	**51-21-1**	**.705**

Once again, the numbers told the story of Michigan's overall performance record against the rivals. Notre Dame was the only rival to hold an edge on Bo and his Wolverines during this era. Coach Schembechler fared very well against Michigan State and Minnesota winning thirty-six of forty-two games. A winning rate of over eighty percent (.800) against two conference rivals is an impressive accomplishment. Bo won two more games against osu and lost two less against the buckeyes compared to the previous twenty-one seasons. He definitely got things back on track in college football's greatest rivalry. Overall, Coach Schembechler ensured that his teams were prepared for their rivals and allowed them to be successful a large majority of the time.

The Rivals - Statistical Summary – 1948-1989

Rival Category	1948-1968	1969-1989
Number of Rival Games	63	73
Number of Rival Wins	26	51
Number of Rival Losses	33	21
Number of Rival Ties	4	1
Rival Win Percentage	.444	.705
Record vs Notre Dame	N/A	4-6-0
Win % vs Notre Dame	N/A	.400
Record vs Minnesota	12-8-1	19-2-0
Win % vs Minnesota	.600	.904
Record vs ohio state	8-12-1	11-9-1
Win % vs ohio state	.405	.547
Record vs Michigan State	6-13-2	17-4-0
Win % vs Michigan State	.333	.810

CHAPTER SEVEN

BO'S HOUSE - THE 1960S

IF BO DIDN'T know about the Three F's" before he arrived in Ann Arbor, it didn't take long for him to learn how important they were to the Michigan Football and the school's entire athletic program. Coaching in the largest college owned football facility in the country brought a little more pressure to the table because attendance was lagging and Don Canham was not going to let it get worse! The buckeyes had been filling their stadium to capacity for years and had led the nation in college football attendance for eleven straight years (1958-1968). Bo knew he had the bigger stadium and it was his job to put winning teams on the field that would help fill it, consistently. Bo would learn very quickly that Mr. Canham wanted his stadium filled for every game, not just for Michigan State, not just for ohio state, but for every game, all the time! Any questions?

Field, Fans, and Finances

I don't know if the conversation ever happened, but I'm pretty certain that Bo and Don Canham must have talked about the fact that the Michigan Athletic Department was losing a lot of money playing in a stadium that was only about seventy percent full for most games. Mr. Canham was a very successful businessman before he took over as Michigan's Athletic Director in 1968. So, losing money was not going to be the pattern during his tenure. The bottom line was pretty simple, Michigan only had one of the three "F's" working. They had the biggest field/stadium in the country, but it had only averaged seventy-two percent of capacity for the last twenty-one years. Fans were voting with their bottoms and their wallets and they were not attending as well as Mr. Canham would like. If tickets were averaging ten dollars a person in those days, then Don Canham had already calculated that they were "losing" more than a quarter of a million dollars (about $282,800) per game. That number projects to over one and one half million dollars during a six-game season. As Bo learned in his very first season, Don Canham would do anything to fill his enormous stadium. And, I mean anything!

Bo knew he had to win games and he had to win the fans. The more games he won, the more fans he would win, so more tickets would be sold and more money would be made for Michigan Athletics. Now, don't misunderstand, Coach Schembechler never made a coaching decision based on "What would the fans think?" that was not his style. But, he understood that his job was pretty simple, just not easy. All he had to do was field winning teams, every year, and fans would support Michigan Football in record numbers, just like they did in the past. Bo knew that filling over one hundred thousand seats was a big deal and now he would play a major role in making it happen.

Of course, Bo was teamed with the greatest athletic director of his time in Don Canham and one of the greatest in the history of college sports. The two of them made a powerful team. Bo was Mr. Inside and it was his job to field winning teams. Canham was Mr. Outside and it was his job to market the program and sell as many tickets as possible for every football game on the schedule. Both men understood their roles and performed them superbly. This dynamic duo took the Michigan Football program to unprecedented levels of success on the field, in the stands, and at the bank. Lets' see how they made it happen.

The Schembechler Era – Year One

Bo Schembechler was a man on a mission in 1969. His stated purpose was to beat ohio state, but there were nine other teams he had to deal with first. His young charges sprinted out of the gate with a twenty-six-point victory (40-14) over Vanderbilt at Michigan Stadium in front of a Band Day crowd of just over seventy thousand people (70,183). Unfortunately, less than fifty thousand fans (49,684) showed up the next week to witness a huge victory (45-7) over Washington as the Wolverines moved to two wins and no losses.

After two games, the Wolverines were averaging over forty-two points per game while only allowing a little over ten points per game. Surprisingly, they were only averaging about sixty-thousand people (59,933) per game compared to just under sixty-four thousand fans (63,944) fans for the first two home games in 1968. The good news was that over sixty-four thousand people (64,476) showed up to watch the ninth ranked Missouri Tigers square off against the unranked Wolverines. The bad news was that Michigan was outplayed in all facets of the game and Missouri rolled to a twenty-three-point (40-17) victory. Bo knew he had some work to do with the Big Ten season ready to start the next week with a home game against Purdue. Which Michigan team would show up and would the fans come out in bigger numbers?

Yes, the fans showed up and so did Bo's Wolverines as a crowd of just over eighty thousand (80,411) witnessed Bo's first Big Ten victory over Purdue (31-20). Thanks to four straight home games, Bo and his Wolverines were looking good with a record of three wins and only one loss, which was exactly the same as Michigan's record in 1968. Attendance was lagging though as the 1968 team drew an average of seventy-five (75,014) fans for their first four games. The 1969 edition was only seeing about sixty-six thousand people (66,205) per game. This is not what Don Canham had in mind.

Things got worse in East Lansing when Duffy showed Bo who was still the boss of college football in the great State of Michigan. Michigan fell short by eleven points (23-12) in East Lansing and I know that Bo did not enjoy the trip home. With five games under his belt, Bo's record stood at three victories and two losses. He was even in the Big Ten with one win and one loss. He still had to navigate through the rest of a tough Big Ten schedule that included three road games out of the next four before finishing at home against the buckeyes. Coach Schembechler's Maize and Blue men tightened their chin straps and went on a four-game winning streak that set them up for the final showdown against osu. This is the game that Bo had pointed towards since his hiring on December 27, 1968. Now it was time to play "The Game of the Century."

Don Canham Sells His Soul to the buckeyes!

Don Canham was pointing to The Big Game" for a different reason. The 1968 Wolverine team drew just over four hundred thousand fans (407,948) to Michigan Stadium which averaged out to just under sixty-eight thousand people (67,991) per game. Through five home games the 1969 Wolverines had drawn a total of about three hundred thousand people (325,192) to Michigan Stadium. This meant thata Michigan drew just over sixty-five thousand fans (65,038) per game in 1969. Mr. Canham needed his biggest crowd of the season to match the 1968 attendance total. However, anyone who knew Don Canham knew that he wanted more, a lot more, and he was going to do whatever it took to get his numbers.

Don Canham got his crowd on November 22, 1969! In fact, it was an NCAA record crowd of over one hundred and three thousand people (103,588). The only problem with this fact was that about twenty-five-thousand were buckeye fans. Remember, I said that Mr. Canham would do anything to fill his enormous stadium, but this was classic. He was desperate for a sellout so, he sold about twenty-four percent of all tickets to the kind folks in columbus. Of course, the buckeye faithful were more than happy to take advantage of this "once in a lifetime" opportunity. Canham probably could have sold thirty-thousand tickets that week to the Scarlet and Gray, but he didn't need to. The buckeyes had to settle for what they got.

As Bob Ufer would say, about five thousand of those tickets went to osu alumni and the other twenty thousand probably went to every truck driver in the state of ohio! The story goes that the Monday after Michigan's big win over the buckeyes, Bo went to Canham's office and told him, "don't you ever do that to me again." Canham's response was something like "I don't think I'll ever have to" and of course, he was right.

Despite the Wolverine's success on the field, attendance didn't spike until the very last game. Don Canham probably breathed a big sigh of relief after the osu game. His "buckeye ticket sale program" pushed the season attendance total to over four hundred and twenty-eight thousand people (428,780) which averaged out to over seventy-one thousand fans (71,463) per game, which was a five percent improvement over 1968. The 1969 "regular season" of Michigan Football ended up exactly the same as the 1968 season with two big differences. First, Michigan defeated the buckeyes for the first time since 1966. Second, they won a share of the Big Ten championship for the first time since 1964. The Bo Schembechler Era was off to a good start.

A Successful First Season – With Room for Improvements

There were lots of plusses in the 1969 season, but both men knew that the biggest room in the Michigan Athletic Department was still the room for improvement. Bo knew he had to win more games and Don Canham knew he had to reduce the "attendance gap" between the season's high and low attendance. Mr. Canham knew he couldn't run a department budget that had a "gap" of nearly fifty-four thousand (53,904 to be exact) and an attendance average of "only" seventy percent (.707). Don Canham didn't want any more crowds of less than fifty thousand, he wanted eighty and ninety thousand at every game except osu and MSU, which he knew would be sold out. Both men knew they had their work cut out for them and they looked forward to the 1970 season with optimism. Don Canham was determined to sell more tickets and improve the bottom line. Bo was focused on getting better on the field – got it?

Coach Schembechler's Michigan Stadium Data Report – Season One 1969

Year*	Games	W-L-T	Attendance	Average	*Capacity	Scored/Avg.	Allowed/Avg.	+/-
1969	6	5-1-0	428,780	71,463	70.7 %	194/32.3	100/16.7	+15.7

*Note – Michigan Stadium capacity was 101,001 in 1969   **Bold Year** = Conference title or tie for the top spot

BO LOVED BEING SURROUNDED BY HIS PLAYERS AND THOSE LEGENDARY WINGED HELMETS.

CHAPTER EIGHT

BO'S HOUSE - THE 1970S

ON JANUARY 1, 1970 no one was sure if Bo would be coaching the Michigan Football team in August or not. His heart attack on the eve of the 1970 Rose Bowl caught a lot of people by surprise, especially Bo. The bad news was that Michigan lost the Rose Bowl to Southern California by a score of 3-10. The good news was that Bo recovered nicely from his heart attack and was on the field again when the Wolverines started the 1970 season. However, nobody was sure how things would play out. There were lots of questions about Bo's health and his ability to keep coaching at the relentless pace that he had done in the past. Wolverine fans were hoping, and praying, that Coach Schembechler would stay on the sidelines for a long time.

The Schembechler Era – 1970 to 1979

The football experts seemed pretty sure that Bo and his Wolverines were for real in 1970. They started the season as the eighth ranked team in the country and posted a solid victory (20-9) against an unranked Arizona team. They won nine straight games and rose to a number four ranking before Bo took his team to Columbus for his first battle against Woody in the horseshoe. Woody had been pointing towards this game from the day that Bo's team knocked them off the road to a national championship in November 1969. Mr. Hayes, and his buckeyes, would get their revenge by a score of 20-9. Season Two of the Bo Era ended up at nine wins and one loss and poll rankings of number nine (AP) and number seven (UPI). Another good season, but still more work to be done.

Bo Goes Streaking

In the next four years (1971-1974) Bo's Footballers averaged over ten wins per season and posted a record of forty-one victories, three defeats, and one tie (41-3-1) which worked out to a winning rate of over ninety-two percent (.922). The Wolverines, and their relentless coach, were on a roll and never lost a game to anyone but the buckeyes during this time period. During this period, Bo's footballers extended a home winning streak that started in 1969 and reached twenty-eight straight games. After the infamous tie (10-10) with the buckeyes in 1973, Michigan increased their "undefeated" streak to forty-one straight home games before they lost a game in Michigan Stadium to, you guessed it, ohio state!

Despite the winning record, attendance didn't grow like Mr. Canham expected. The good news was that attendance increased by over thirteen percent (13.6) from 1970 to 1974. Instead of averaging about seventy-nine thousand fans per game (79,361) Michigan now saw over ninety-three thousand people (93,600) at every home contest.

The 1972 team snapped ohio state's fourteen-year streak of leading the nation in football attendance when they drew an average of over eighty-five thousand fans per game (85,566) compared to ohio's eight-four thousand (84,903). The buckeyes came back in 1973 to win the "attendance" battle, for the last time.

The good news was that the 1974 Wolverines were first in national attendance average with an average of over ninety-three fans per game (93,684) and continued to lead the buckeyes and the nation in attendance for the rest of Bo's tenure. The bad news was that the 1974 Wolverines "only" averaged about ninety-two percent (.921) percent of capacity. I'm certain that Mr. Canham was wondering what he and his fantastic football coach had to do to fill Michigan Stadium on a more regular basis. Despite their incredible winning record, the Wolverines were still averaging about eight thousand empty seats per game and losing nearly a million dollars a season in lost ticket revenues.

In 1972 Title IX legislation was signed into law by President Richard M. Nixon. This law prohibited sex discrimination in any education program or activity (including HS and college sports) within an institution receiving any type of federal financial assistance. Efforts to circumvent the law failed in 1974. In June of 1975, Title IX was here to stay and school officials were given three years to comply. Universities around the country would have to provide equal numbers of sports for men and women and athletic directors would have to figure out a way to pay for them. I am sure that Don Canham felt no financial pressure at the start of the 1975 season, absolutely no pressure at all.

College Football's Greatest Attendance Streak Begins

The 1975 edition of Wolverine football, Bo's seventh at Michigan, was noteworthy for a number of reasons. It was the first time since 1969 that the Wolverines didn't win at least nine games and the first time in four years that they didn't win at least ten games. Bo's Michigan Men slipped to a record of eight wins, two losses and two ties (8-2-2) and finished in second place in the conference. Although he might have been disappointed with the final record, Don Canham must have been thrilled with what happened in the stands.

Team Ninety-Six of the Michigan Football tradition played seven home games and four of them were in front of one hundred thousand people or more. Only two Michigan Football teams had ever played in front of two home crowds of over one hundred thousand people (1957 and 1974). On October 25, 1975, a Homecoming Crowd of over ninety-three thousand people (93,857) witnessed a blowout victory (55-7) over the Indiana Hoosiers. This game was significant because it would be the last time the Wolverines played in front of a home crowd of less than one hundred thousand people. Yes, that was a very long time ago! A crowd of over one hundred and two thousand people (102,415) showed up on November 8, 1975 to witness a shutout victory (28-0) over Purdue. This was the start of an attendance streak that continued through the rest of Bo Era and beyond. Michigan has played in front of a crowd of at least one hundred thousand college football fans since that landmark day.

It was a streak that Don Canham had been working towards since 1968. Bo's ultra-successful football team would become the "cash cow" that would generate more revenue than ever! The increased financial burden of the Title IX legislation meant that Mr. Canham needed every penny to run his athletic department. The 1975 season set the stage for the great things that were to come. More importantly, it helped to ease the coming financial burden of Title IX in Ann Arbor.

In the decade of the seventies Bo's Wolverines averaged over nine wins per season, posted the best regular season record of the decade (96-10-3) and won almost ninety percent (.894) of their games. At home, Michigan was almost unbeatable. Bo's home record in the 1970's was an incredible fifty-nine victories, four defeats and three ties (59-4-3) which worked out to a winning percentage of ninety-two percent. His teams posted seven undefeated home seasons in this decade and made Michigan Stadium "Bo's House" before it became the "Big House." The Wolverines won ten games in seven of the seasons of the decade and also won, or tied, for seven Big Ten championships.

A Strong Start, but a Weak Finish

Although Michigan bolted out of the gate in 1970, and played at incredible level for most of the decade, the 1979 team did not finish as strong as Bo would like. Bo's teams had steam rolled just about every team on the schedule, except the buckeyes, through 1978. In 1979 the Wolverines finished with eight wins and four losses which wasn't terrible, but definitely not up to Bo's standards.

One thing that was particularly bothersome was the fact that the Wolverines lost two games at home for the first time in Bo's tenure (5-2-0 overall) and finished the season, and the decade, on a three- game losing streak thanks to a 17-15 loss to North Carolina in the Gator Bowl.

Off the field, Bo had some serious health challenges that complicated his efforts to coach "his way" during the decade. Bo survived a heart attack (1969) and a quadruple heart by-pass surgery (1976) during this time. He had literally put his heart and soul into the Michigan Football program and the efforts produced amazing results, but maybe the price was too high.

History tells us that Bo started taking better care of himself during the late 1970's because he realized that his incredible work ethic was taking a toll on his health. Fortunately, he came out of the seventies in good health and assembled a strong medical team that would help him stay healthy for another decade as the head man at Michigan.

116

Coach Schembechler's Michigan Stadium Data Report – The 1970s

Year*	W-L-T	Attendance	Average	*Capacity	Scored/Avg.	Allowed/Avg	+/-
1970	6-0-0	476,164	79,361	78.5%	204/34.0	52/8.7	+25.3
1971	7-0-0	564,376	80,625	79.7%	309/44.1	27/3.9	+40.3
1972	6-0-0	513,398	85,566	84.7%	144/24.0	20/3.3	+20.7
1973	6-0-1	595,171	85,024	83.6%	200/28.6	45/6.4	+22.1
1974	6-0-0	562,105	93,684	92.1%	228/38.0	14/2.3	+35.7
1975	4-1-2	689,146	98,449	96.8%	230/32.9	68/9.7	+23.2
1976	7-0-0	722,113	103,159	101.4%	317/45.3	58/8.2	+37.0
1977	7-0-0	729,418	104,203	102.5%	232/33.1	51/7.2	+25.9
1978	5-1-0	629,697	104,948	103.2%	185/30.8	57/9.5	+21.3
1979	5-2-0	730,315	104,331	102.6%	214/30.6	86/12.3	+18.3
Totals	59-4-3	621,190	93,935	92.6%	2263/34.3	478/7.2	+27.1

*Note – Michigan Stadium capacity was increased to 101,701 in 1973. **Bold Year** = Conference title or tie

Michigan's Dynamic Duo

Attendance didn't grow as quickly as Mr. Canham wanted. However, it grew steadily during the decade of the 1970's. The Wolverines were setting national attendance records for single games and seasons on a regular basis. More importantly, they were getting more consistent in their attendance patterns and closing the gap between the crowd "highs" and "lows." By the end of the decade the "attendance gap" was "only" about five thousand five hundred fans (5,465 to be exact) versus over thirty-seven thousand (37,391) in 1970.

Canham's marketing genius, and Bo's winning teams, produced results that were unprecedented in college football history. Michigan now had the perfect combination of the three F's. The **F**ield (Michigan Stadium) was the biggest in the nation, the **F**ans were coming out in record numbers and filling the gigantic stadium beyond capacity for every game. Of course, the **F**inances created by the "Dynamic Duo" of Don Canham and Bo Schembechler were significant. Michigan was leading the nation in season attendance and average attendance per game and breaking many records along the way. The bottom line was that Bo and Don Canham were doing great things together and everything was good in Ann Arbor.

BO AND DON CANHAM RECEIVE A PAINTING OF A MICHIGAN WOLVERINE IN 1975.

CHAPTER NINE

BO'S HOUSE - THE 1980S

AFTER ELEVEN YEARS on the job there wasn't a lot of mystery about what you could expect from a Bo Schembechler football team. Things were even easier to predict when the Wolverines played in Michigan Stadium. The defense would be tough, almost punishing at times, so opponents weren't going to score a lot of points. Special teams would be very good and the offense would be effective, but maybe a tad boring for some Michigan fans. However, the option offense that Bo used for his first eleven seasons was starting to sputter a little by the end of the 1979 season. (Remember, they lost the last three games of the 1979 season.)

A Slow Start in the 1980s

The Wolverines started the decade of the eighties with a narrow victory (17-10) over Northwestern in the season opener at Michigan Stadium. Bo's Michigan Men lost (29-27) at Notre Dame on Harry Oliver's miracle field goal on the last play of the game. Michigan had now lost four times in the last five contests going back to 1979 – unacceptable! Bo had seen enough, so, he made a decision the next day that was probably made only once in the history of Michigan football – he changed the offense after two games into a season. Wow, was he crazy, desperate, or brilliant? It was probably a little bit of all three as he made the decision to scrap the option offense and go with a power running game and some play action passing. He did have a pretty good quarterback named John Wangler, who liked to throw the ball to a guy named Anthony Carter, so maybe Bo wasn't insane after all. Coach Schembechler also had a great offensive line and three excellent backs to carry the pigskin. Maybe this crazy idea just might work.

With only six days to install a new offense, the results were predictable when the seventeenth ranked Wolverines hosted an unranked South Carolina team. The Gamecocks came away with a hard- fought victory (17-14). Michigan had the pleasure of meeting a hard-to-tackle running back named George Rogers, who would go on to win the Heisman Trophy that season.

Bo and his Wolverines were sitting on a two-game losing streak, had lost five of their last six games over two seasons, and some critics were asking whether it was time for the Michigan coach to consider retirement. Things were looking bleak in Ann Arbor as the Wolverines fought to get back on track. They got things rolling in the right direction with a big win (38-13) over California and the streak was on.

Bo's Michigan Men won nine straight games after the South Carolina loss, finished a perfect 8-0 in the Big Ten, and won an undisputed conference championship. Oh yes, Bo's players gave him something that a Bo coached team had never done before. Team number 101 gave their beloved coach his first bowl victory - a dominating win (23-6) over Washington in the 1981 Rose Bowl. The Wolverines finished fourth in the polls, but Bo believed his Wolverines could have beaten anyone at the end of the season. He was probably right.

The "new" offense became a dominating force as they led the nation in rushing with over two hundred fifty yards per game (251.9). It showed a lot of balance with just over one hundred and forty passing yards (140.3) per game as well. The defense stepped up during the winning streak as they shut out three teams and did not allow a touchdown in twenty-two consecutive quarters. Bo and his team had worked through a funk like none he had ever faced in his coaching career. Year one of the decade of the eighties was now in the books and everyone was wondering how good the Wolverines would be in the next few years.

Michigan started the 1981 season as the number one team in college football, but that didn't last very long as they lost their home opener/Big Ten opener to an unranked Wisconsin team (21-14). The Wolverines would win nine games that season, but they finished with six wins and three losses in the Big Ten with late seasons losses to Iowa (9-7) and ohio state (14-9). They did win the Bluebonnet Bowl in Houston against UCLA (33-14) which was their second consecutive bowl victory after losing seven straight games. It was also the first time that the Wolverines won two bowl games in the same calendar year. The Wolverines third place conference finish was their second in the last three years and some people were wondering if Bo was slipping.

One thing that wasn't slipping was Michigan's home football attendance. The incredible streak of one hundred-thousand-person crowds continued into the 1980's and is still going today. Michigan averaged over one hundred and two percent of capacity and athletic department finances were growing steadily. Bo's winning ways and the marketing genius of Don Canham combined to create a powerfully positive synergy that could not be stopped. The NCAA football attendance records were being broken regularly in Ann Arbor and nobody else was even close.

Bo is Tempted by Texas A & M

Apparently, Texas A & M didn't think that Bo was slipping as an A & M regent/millionaire started to "recruit" Bo right after the Bluebonnet Bowl in Houston. The Aggies were looking for the right man to be the next coach and athletic director in College Station, Texas. At the time, Bo was making about sixty thousand dollars a year at Michigan and the A & M offer was almost four times that amount for ten years! Bum Bright, led an aggressive effort to bring Bo to Texas that included very big bucks, cars, country club memberships, expense accounts, you name it. Bo and his family would have been set for life.

On January 15, 1982 Bo announced that he was staying at Michigan. He had carefully weighed the pros and cons of the A & M situation and concluded that it was really about the money. Bo decided that loyalty to his players and to Michigan meant more to him than anything else Yes, he pretty much declared himself a "Wolverine" for life that day.

Coach Schembechler actually got a nice pay raise out of it. Domino's Pizza magnate, Tom Monaghan, threw in a Domino's Pizza franchise to boot – in downtown columbus, ohio. I wonder what folks in buckeye nation were thinking when they learned that Bo would be selling pizza in Woody's back yard! Bo was almost embarrassed by all the attention and the distractions that these "informal" meetings and discussions had caused. He was glad to get it behind him so he could get back to focusing on what was most important – Michigan Football!

Bo and Canham Drift Apart

The only down side to the whole A & M affair was that the process strained the relationship between Bo and Don Canham. Bo wasn't really looking for a job at the time, he thought he had a pretty good one at Michigan. Initially, he was probably flattered, then flabbergasted that someone would offer him the kind of money that Mr. Bright was talking about. He would have been the highest paid coach/athletic director in college football. Don Canham may have thought that Bo was just looking for a raise. We'll never know and it really didn't matter in the great scheme of things, but it did change things between Bo and his boss. As Bo related in his first book with Mitch Albom, "*BO*", "...We (Bo and Canham) drifted further apart after that. I went my way, he went his. We didn't fight, but we didn't spend much time together either. We never socialized."

Another sensitive item between Bo and Don Canham surfaced in the eighties as well. Mr. Canham had been on the NCAA Television Committee for many years and he and Bo differed greatly on this issue. Canham's take on television and football was pretty simple. The networks could pretty much do anything they wanted to do to increase the exposure of college football and increase the revenues that were paid to universities that fielded NCAA Division I football teams.

Bo's take was a lot different. He believed that the game of college football should be played the way it was intended to be played. To Bo that meant that "toe meets leather at 1:00 pm in the afternoon" – game on. If the television people wanted to broadcast the games they were invited for the one o'clock kickoff. Bo was not in favor of moving kickoff times to get more television exposure or more money.

Obviously, this "old fashioned" view did not keep up with the times and Bo pretty much got crushed on this one. The 1985 game between Michigan and Ohio State in the Big House was pushed back to a 3:30 pm kickoff which meant that the game would end in the dark. Canham must have gotten some perks to make this happen because somebody had to pay for the portable lighting that was set up for the game. The Wolverines won the game, but I know Bo was not happy with the undue influence of the television networks on his beloved game.

The Wolverines came back nicely in 1982 as they won Bo's tenth conference championship with a record of eight wins and one loss. Overall, they won eight games and lost four which included a non-conference home loss to UCLA and road losses to Notre Dame and ohio state. Michigan ended the season in the Rose Bowl with a second loss to UCLA and finished as the fifteenth ranked team in the UPI poll.

The 1983 Wolverines won more games and ended the season with a record of 9 wins and 3 losses. They earned a second-place tie in the Big Ten with a conference record of eight wins and one loss. Their only loss was a ten-point defeat at Illinois (16-6). The Fighting Illini won the Big Ten Championship that year with a perfect conference record of nine wins and no losses.

Bo's Worst Season

The 1984 season started off beautifully for Bo and his fourteenth ranked Wolverines as they upset the top ranked Miami Hurricanes in Ann Arbor by eight points (22-14). They rose to number three in the rankings the next week, but lost to the sixteenth ranked Washington Huskies (20-11). Michigan bounced back with consecutive victories over Wisconsin and Indiana before hosting the Michigan State at Michigan Stadium. The Wolverines suffered two losses that day. First, they lost their quarterback when Jim Harbaugh broke his arm trying to recover a fumble early in the game and then they lost the game to their in-state rivals (19-7). Ouch & Ouch!

Things were looking bleak in Ann Arbor with Harbaugh out for the season, but Bo had faith in his young team and he focused on getting Chris Zurbrugg ready for his first start. Michigan won the next week with an impressive win over Northwestern (31-0) and left the Homecoming crowd with some hope that the season might turn out okay.

Unfortunately, the Wolverines lost four of the last six games to finish the 1984 regular season with six victories and five defeats (6-5-0) for sixth place in the conference (5-4-0) which would be Bo's worst conference finish ever! They almost upset the number one ranked Brigham Young Cougars in the Holiday Bowl, but eventually lost by seven points (24-17). The final record finished with six wins and six losses, (6-6-0) easily Bo's worst season in his entire coaching career.

One of the best Bo stories ever told resulted from this dismal season. It was told by Michigan's iconic equipment manager, Jon Falk, in his book, "*If These Walls Could Talk.*" It was a frigid, snowy, night in January 1985 and Jon Falk was driving, very slowly, down I-94 headed for Detroit. He was on the outskirts of Ann Arbor when he saw a man trying to hitch a ride. He thought the man looked familiar, but wasn't sure. As the man got closer, he was wearing a blue "M" hat, just like the one Bo always wore. As Falk got closer to the man, he could see a car behind him that looked just like Bo's car. Falk pulled over and walked towards the shivering man and discovered that it was Bo!

Bo was freezing on the outside, but man was he hot on the inside. He was trying to get to the airport for a recruiting trip. He told Falk to take him to the airport – now! As Falk started his trip with the frozen coach, Bo started to rant about the fact that he had been standing on the side of the road for about forty-five minutes and not one person had bothered to stop and help. What really ticked him off was the fact that three State Trooper vehicles had cruised right on by the stranded coach. Falk's reply was classic. He said, "Well Bo, you gotta remember now, you were only six and six last year." Bo forced a smile, he knew that Falk had him, what could he say, except "get me to the airport Falk!"

Bo Gets the Wolverines Back on Track

The Wolverines had a healthy quarterback in 1985 and Jim Harbaugh, along with his talented teammates, was on a mission to make people forget what happened in 1984. Michigan started the season unranked, but rose to number two in the country after five straight victories. Their biggest test of the season matched them against Hayden Fry's number one ranked Iowa Hawkeyes and his pink visitor's locker room. Bo had Jon Falk line the locker room walls with white butcher paper, every inch of it, but it didn't matter. The Wolverines didn't allow a touchdown, but lost a heart breaker as the Hawkeyes won by two points on a last-minute field goal (12-10).

Michigan would not lose another game that season although they did tie Illinois (3-3) in Champaign in early November. They finished with a victory (27-23) over an eighth ranked Nebraska team and ended the season as the number two ranked team in both the UPI and AP polls. Although the Wolverines did not win the Big Ten title, maybe Bo found some consolation with his highest finish ever in the polls.

One important fact that a lot of people might have been overlooking was the three year "title drought" that just ended. This was the third straight season that Michigan did not win or share the Big Ten championship which meant that Bo had not yet kept his promise of "Those Who Stay Will Be Champions" to the Juniors on this team. There was no pressure here, but it was hard to ignore that message when the sign hung right over the entry door to Bo's office area and in the locker room. There was always pressure to win at Michigan, but the 1986 team had to be wondering if they would be the first group of players in the Bo Era not to win a Big Ten Championship.

Bo made sure that his players knew the team goals (Beat ohio state, win the Big Ten and win the Rose Bowl) for the 1986 season. The Wolverines got the message. They finished with a record of eleven wins and two losses (11-2-0). They achieved two of the three goals with a two-point win (26-24) at osu and Bo's eleventh Big Ten title (tie), but came up short in the Rose Bowl with a tough loss (22-15) loss to John Cooper and his Arizona State Sun Devils. Bo kept his promise to the Class of 1986, they were Big Ten Champions for the first time and he had to figure out what to do with eleven rings!

Bo's Biggest Disappointment

In addition to the ring challenge, Bo was faced with what he called "the single biggest off-field disappointment of my football career." He was referring to his dealings with two former players who signed with sports agents during their senior year and then lied about it when Bo questioned them later.

Bo did everything he could possibly do to inform his players, adhere to the NCAA eligibility rules and keep them from being hurt by the agents. Garland Rivers and Bob Perryman fell prey to the tactics of some shrewd sports agents and paid the price. They lost a true friend who could have helped them down the road and Bo never spoke to either player again.

The 1987 edition of the Michigan Wolverines had a strong returning cast that included a returning All-American, John Elliott and a potential one in Mark Messner. Bo knew he had to settle on a quarterback to replace All-American Jim Harbaugh, but things were looking pretty good for the Maize and Blue. The media had them as a ninth ranked team when they played the sixteenth ranked Irish in Ann Arbor, but it wasn't even close as the Irish spanked the Wolverines by nineteen points (26-7), ouch!

The Wolverines won the next three games and managed to climb back to number fourteen in the rankings before Bo and his boys traveled to Michigan State. The Spartans were ready and the Wolverines were not. The Green and White won by six points (17-11) and Bo was probably thinking back to 1969, the last time he lost a road game in East Lansing.

The unranked Wolverines returned home to blow out Iowa (37-10) and the question became "which team would show up at Indiana next week?" Bo's good Wolverines or not so good Wolverines?" Bill Mallory, a friend of Bo's for many years, was working hard to build a winning tradition at Indiana and Bo didn't help him much – Mallory had lost his first three games against Michigan. The fourth matchup was a charm for Coach Mallory and his Hoosiers as they sent Bo and his Wolverines back to Ann Arbor to contemplate a four-point loss (14-10).

After seven games Michigan was looking pretty "average" with four wins and three losses. They managed to win the next three games against, Northwestern, Minnesota and Illinois. The Wolverines were now looking better (7-3-0) and appeared to be ready for the buckeyes. Unfortunately, they lost by three lousy points to their bitter rivals in the Big House (23-20).

Bo's Surprise Surgery

That was the last game Bo would coach in 1987 even though Michigan was selected to play Alabama in the Hall of Fame Bowl. In early December, Bo was in the hospital for a catheterization procedure and he started feeling a little funny. He told his wife Millie that he thought he was having a heart attack. Within minutes Coach Schembechler was going to have his second quadruple heart by-pass surgery and he wasn't sure how it would all turn out.

Bo wondered if this was it and later told "*Bo*" author Mitch Albom, "That one, I thought, would be the clincher." Bo had a simple request, "God, just let me live." Bo's heart was getting older and less dependable. He figured that he would be lucky to be walking, but wondered if he would ever coach again.

Bo made it again as his heart surgeon, Dr. Otto Gago, performed another miraculous procedure. By January 2, 1988, he was recovering nicely in Ann Arbor. Meanwhile, acting Head Coach, Gary Moeller took Michigan to Tampa, Florida to play in the Hall of Fame Bowl. Coach Moeller, the staff and his players gave Bo something to smile about – an exciting victory over Alabama, maybe too exciting for Bo's delicate heart. The Wolverines won by four points (28-24) and Michigan finished with eight wins and four losses for the season and a number nineteen ranking in the Associated Press poll.

Bo Gets Another Hat to Wear

As if he didn't have enough on his plate, Bo was appointed as the Michigan Athletic Director in July 1988 while remaining as the Head Football Coach. Originally, he said "no" to the job because Michigan wanted Bo to drop coaching and just be the athletic director. Bo declined because he wanted to "coach" more than he wanted to "direct." When the second offer was made, it was clear that Bo would be able to coach and be the athletic director. Technically, he could look his boss in the mirror every morning so the only person who could fire Bo was Bo. Now Bo was wearing two very important hats and he must have thought if it all might be too much for him and his weary heart. Could he do justice to both jobs? How much of a toll would the added responsibilities take on his health, would he lose his edge?

As it turned out, he assembled a strong staff in the athletic department and leaned on his assistant coaches a little more, but kept enough "edge" to be very effective. He would continue to be leader of his beloved football team and find the time he needed to move the athletic department forward as well. Besides, Bo thought he was superman and he truly believed that he could, and would, do justice to both jobs.

Wolverines Bounce Back in 1988

Coach Schembechler and his Wolverines had another strong core of returning players who wanted to improve on their record (8-4-0) and fourth place conference finish in 1987. Michigan was ranked number nine in the country when they went to Notre Dame, but lost by two precious points (19-17). The fifteenth ranked Wolverines hosted the number one Miami Hurricanes the following week and gave them all they could handle before losing a one point heartbreaker (31-30). The Wolverines had never started with two straight losses under Coach Schembechler although he did lose his first two at Miami of Ohio to start the 1965 season. His Redskins bounced back to win the Mid-American Conference title that year. Could the Wolverines duplicate such a feat?

Even at zero wins and two losses, the pollsters thought Michigan was still a pretty good football team and it turned out that they were right. The nineteenth ranked Wolverines hosted an unranked Wake Forest team and won by ten points (19-9), Nothing spectacular, but a step in the right direction. Michigan would get better and better as the weeks went on. By the time they played ohio state they were ranked twelfth in the country and had to fight off their unranked rivals before they won by three points (34-31) in Columbus. The Wolverines finished with a conference record of seven wins, no losses and one tie (7-0-1) and gave Bo his twelfth conference title. Michigan was undefeated in their last ten games (9-0-1) and finished the season with an impressive eight-point victory in the Rose Bowl (22-14) over the USC Trojans. Their final record of nine wins, two losses and one tie (9-2-1) allowed them to finish the season as the fourth ranked team in the AP and UPI polls.

The Rocket Blasts Off Twice to Beat Bo

The 1989 season started off with bowl game level hoopla as the second ranked Wolverines hosted Lou Holtz and his number one Irish. Unfortunately, for Bo and his Michigan Men, Notre Dame came away with a narrow victory (24-19). This was the third year in a row that Lou had bested Bo and it was getting old. This was the game that had not one, but two, Raghib "Rocket" Ismail kickoff returns. Bo blamed himself for not squib kicking on the second return as his assistant coaches had recommended. Two kickoff returns by the same player in the same game never happened before in Michigan Football History - probably won't happen again. Yet, it happened to Bo that September Day. Ugh!

Bo got his team ready for a tough test the next week as they traveled to Los Angeles to play UCLA in the Rose Bowl – the stadium, not the game. Michigan won a squeaker by one point (24-23) and then beat Maryland by twenty points (41-21) to get ready for the Big Ten gauntlet.

The Wolverines would run the table in conference play and finish with a perfect record of eight victories and no defeats. A convincing victory (28-18) over ohio state at the Big House gave Bo his second consecutive conference title and thirteenth overall. As Bo, walked off the field after the twenty-first edition of the Michigan vs osu game, he knew that he had coached his last game in Michigan Stadium. (Note – the great Fielding Yost won undisputed conference titles in his last two seasons as well.)

Bo's Big Announcement

Within the next few weeks only his AD, his wife and Jon Falk, his trusted equipment manager, knew that he was going to retire after the Rose Bowl game. Eventually, he told his staff, players and the world. He would "officially" retire from coaching and turn his beloved team over to his trusted assistant, Gary Moeller, on January 2, 1990. He was adamant that there was going to be no big hype about winning one for Bo and all that stuff. He just wanted his team to play good Michigan Football and let the chips fall where they may.

As it turned out, the chips didn't quite fall the way Bo would have liked, but what else could he expect? Bowl games and bad calls probably did as much to put the wear and tear on Bo's heart as anything he did in coaching. The fourth quarter "phantom holding call," after a brilliant fake punt, paved the way for USC's final touchdown as the Bo and his Wolverines went down to another disappointing Rose Bowl defeat (17-10).

After twenty-one years at the helm, it was over. Bo's five-year handshake lasted sixteen years beyond the original "agreement." Don Canham told me in a meeting in 1986 that hiring Bo was "the best decision I ever made" and it was pretty hard to argue otherwise. Bo's impact on the Michigan Football program was significant and long lasting. Bo's Wolverines posted some impressive numbers in the 1980's, but they were not as dominant as they were in the 1970's. Bo's overall record in the eighties was ninety wins, twenty-nine losses and two ties (90-29-2) for a winning rate of over seventy-five percent (.756). Bo continued to be very difficult to beat at home as his Maize and Blue men won fifty-two times in sixty-two games for a winning percentage of almost eight-four percent (.839).

Coach Schembechler's Michigan Stadium Data Report – The 1980-1989

Year*	W-L-T	Attendance	Average	*Capacity	Scored/Avg.	Allowed/Avg.	+/-
1980	5-1-0	625,861	104,310	102.6%	167/27.8	77/12.8	+15.0
1981	4-2-0	632,990	105,499	104.3%	170/28.3	67/11.1	+17.2
1982	5-1-0	631,743	105,291	103.5%	206/34.3	102/17.0	+17.3
1983	6-0-0	626,916	104,486	102.7%	180/30.0	79/13.2	+16.8
1984	5-2-0	726,734	103,819	102.1%	148/21.1	92/13.1	+8.0
1985	6-0-0	633,530	105,588	103.8%	189/31.5	50/8.3	+23.2
1986	6-0-0	631,261	105,210	103.5%	184/30.7	86/14.3	+16.4
1987	5-2-0	731,281	104,460	102.7%	235/33.6	83/11.9	+21.7
1988	5-1-0	628,807	104,801	103.0%	157/26.2	65/10.8	+15.3
1989	5-1-0	632,135	105,356	103.6%	192/32.0	100/16.7	+15.3
Totals	**52-10-0**	**650,126**	**104,882**	**103.1%**	**1828/29.5**	**801/12.9**	**+16.6**

*Note – Michigan Stadium capacity was 101,701 for the entire decade   **Bold Year** = Conference title or tie

The chart above summarizes the numbers that Bo's teams posted in the last decade of his illustrious coaching career at Michigan. He also won five more Big Ten titles during the decade. The numbers were strong on both sides of the ball, but they just were not as good as they were in the Seventies. Scoring was down a little, and points allowed went up quite a bit for the defensive-minded Schembechler. The point differentials were very positive, except for 1984. Overall, a very strong body of work, but not the legendary resume that Bo's teams compiled from 1970 to 1979.

Attendance during the last ten years of Bo's tenure was absolutely amazing. The "average" crowd for the decade was almost one hundred and five thousand fans per game (104,882) which was three percent over capacity. More importantly, the "attendance gap" had completely shifted from an underachieving status to an overachieving status. Attendance still varied from game to game, but the question was not "will we fill the stadium today?" – it was "how full was it?" At the end of the decade of the eighties the average crowd variance was not quite three thousand fans per game (2,894), but every game was an "over capacity-sellout." Amazing!

Bo's winning ways helped Michigan lead the nation in attendance for seventeen of his twenty-one years at the helm. The Wolverines finished with a streak of sixteen straight years as the national attendance leader under Bo's leadership. Michigan averaged ninety-six percent of capacity during his twenty-one-year tenure. When Don Canham retired as Athletic Director in 1988 he knew that he and his amazing coach set a standard that would continue for a long time to come. It took a little longer than Mr. Canham wanted to, but once the "pump was primed" it started flowing and it's still going strong to this day!

Bo's House

Bo's won-lost record at "home" (115-16-3) and his winning percentage (.869) are the best in Michigan Stadium history. I like to refer to The Big House as Bo's House because he was almost unbeatable in Michigan's legendary stadium. Coach Schembechler's teams posted ten undefeated home seasons in twenty-one years at Michigan Stadium and he never lost more than two home games in any season. Bo's ten undefeated home seasons, again, put him behind the legendary Yost who had fifteen in his twenty-five years at the helm. Bo's teams won thirteen Big Ten championships which is the best in Michigan Football history and tied him with his "Football Father," Woody Hayes, for the most in conference history.

<u>Bo's House Totals – 1969-1989</u>

Year(s)	W-L-T	Attendance	Average	Capacity	Scored/Avg	Allowed/Avg	+/-
1969	5-1-0	428,780	71,463	70.7 %	194/32.3	100/16.7	+15.7
1970s	59-4-3	6,199,710	93,935	92.6 %	2263/34.3	478/7.2	+27.1
1980s	51-11-0	6,502,684	104,882	103.1 %	1828/29.5	801/12.9	+16.6
Totals	115-16-3	13,131,174	98,994	96.6 %	4479/33.4	1379/10.3	+23.1

In addition, his Michigan Men averaged over thirty-three points (33.4) per game in Michigan Stadium while only allowing about ten points (10.3) points per game. The positive point differential of over twenty-three points per game (+23.1) made it pretty likely that Michigan fans would not only see a victory at Michigan Stadium, but that it would probably be a "whuppin" as they say in Kentucky. Bo's defense was no slouch either as they posted thirty-two shutouts in Ann Arbor, but his teams always scored at least six points in all his games in Ann Arbor.

A Closer Look at Homecoming

Bo never had much fun talking about bowl games and he was the first to tell you that his bowl record wasn't very good. He never made excuses, just acknowledged the facts and always thought about playing in and winning the "next bowl" game instead of focusing too much on the past. Homecoming, however, had to be one of his favorite topics. No one in the history of Michigan Football (who coached in more than three Homecoming games) ever did what Bo did. He won every Homecoming game he coached – amazing!

Bo's perfect record of twenty-one Homecoming victories, no defeats and no ties (21-0-0) meant that millions of Michigan Alumni went home happy after their Homecoming visit during his twenty-one- year run. Coach Schembechler's stellar Homecoming record stands above all others, Yost, Kipke, Crisler, Oosterbaan, and everyone else past, present and probably future. If Bo could have captured that "Homecoming Magic" and saved some for the bowl games, who knows what would have happened? Of course, the "Homecoming Magic" stayed in Ann Arbor and didn't Bo much good in any other places. However, it would be hard to argue that anybody, anytime, anywhere was better on Homecoming than Glenn Edward "Bo" Schembechler. Got it?

A Little Bit About Defense

Everyone knows that Bo took great pride in his defenses and without getting into too much detail I want to share some interesting numbers about Bo's defenses. As we have seen, Bo's numbers were very good on offense and defense. However, one stat we haven't discussed yet is shutouts. Bo's first defense posted one shutout in 1969 and exploded to thirty-one in the 70s. His defensive numbers were down in the 80's, but they still included thirteen more shutouts for a total of forty-four. Bo's teams were only shut out twice, both on the road – once in the 70s (16-0 at the Minnesota Mud Bowl) and at Iowa (26-0) in 1984.

Overall, Bo's teams had at least one shutout in eighteen of his twenty-one seasons. His 1976 team had five shutouts including the masterpiece (22-0) at Columbus. Three teams (1972, 1974, and 1978) recorded four shutouts in a season. Bo's defenses posted three shutouts in five more seasons (1970, 1971, 1973 [3 straight], 1980 [3 straight], and 1985). Yes, Bo had some great defensive coordinators who knew how important good defense was to a winning football program and they gave him plenty to smile about on most football Saturdays!

Coaching Records at Michigan Stadium – 1927-1989

Years	Coach	Games	W-L-T	Win %	Avg. Attend.	% Capacity
1927-28	Wieman	11	8-3-0	.727	51,607	60.1%
1929-37	Kipke	51	31-16-4	.647	33,829	39.4%
1938-47	Crisler	58	46-9-3	.819	52,223	60.8%
1948-58	Oosterbaan	67	46-19-2	.701	76,163	78.1%
1958-68	Elliott	61	33-26-2	.557	68,436	67.8%
1969-89	Bo	134	115-16-3	.869	98,994	96.6%

Michigan Stadium Statistical Summary 1948-1989

Category	1948-1968	1969-1989
Number of Home Games	131	134
Number of Home Wins	77	115
Number of Home Losses	48	16
Number of Home Ties	6	3
Home Winning %	.610	.869
NCAA Attendance Leader	4	17
NCAA Attendance Leader Streak	2	16
Average Crowd Size	70,970	98,077
Average % of Capacity	.720	.960
Most Home Wins/Season	6 (2x)	7 (3x)
Most Home Losses/Season	4 (4x)	2 (4x)
Undefeated Home Seasons	2	10
Longest Home Win Streak	9	28
Longest Home Undefeated Streak	9	41
Longest Home Losing Streak	5	2 (2x)
Home Game Scoring Average	19.3	30.9
Home Points Allowed Average	13.6	10.3
Average Home Point Differential	+5.7	+20.5
Home Shutouts Posted	17	32
Home Games – Did Not Score	10	0
Homecoming Games	21	21
Homecoming Games Won	15	21
Homecoming Games Lost	6	0
Homecoming Game Win %	.710	1.000

BO LEADS HIS TEAM ONTO THE FIELD FOR ANOTHER MEDIA DAY.

CHAPTER TEN

BO'S MICHIGAN LEGACY

BY THE END of his coaching career, Coach Schembechler had some football coaching accomplishments that put him in a very elite class. At the time of his retirement, he had the most wins of any active coach and his 234 career wins at Miami of Ohio and Michigan was fifth best in college football history. Only four men were ahead of him, all legends - guys like Stagg, Bryant, Pop Warner, and that guy named Hayes. So, the man who was the second choice in December 1968 worked out okay. He exceeded all expectations except for maybe his own. He had a few regrets (bowl record and no national title), but that's about it. He established a winning program that was admired and respected for its integrity and adherence to the "rules." Bo didn't learn the tricks of the coaching trade, he just learned the trade. Glenn Edward Schembechler did all the hard work that it took to build something very special at Michigan from 1969 to 1989.

From the first day he put on his Athletic Director's hat, Bo made it clear that he would focus on the Fourth "**F**" – **F**acilities. Specifically, he wanted to build a first-class football training facility that would take Michigan Football into the 21st Century. This would become a personal challenge for Bo and he was off and running in July 1988 with an aggressive fund-raising program. Bo was focused on raising over twelve million dollars to build what he envisioned as the Center of Champions – a place that Michigan Football players, coaches and staff would call "home" for decades to come. He knew that Michigan had a championship level stadium, but the practice facilities needed work. So, that became his focus. When it was all said and done, Bo left the Michigan Football Program in excellent shape with a ton of quality players ready to go for his friend Gary Moeller. Bo set a very high standard and now we would see if coach Moeller could do as well.

I believe that every leader has three primary missions. First, he must give the organization the very best he has for as long as he is employed. Second, he needs to leave the organization in better shape than when he arrived. Finally, he needs to develop his followers so, they can carry on successfully when he leaves.

I would say that Bo succeeded beyond expectations in all three areas. He gave Michigan everything he had and the results he helped to produce were right up there with the legendary Yost and the rest of the great coaches at Michigan. Bo enhanced the tradition of Wolverine Football and he improved the program in every measurable way except the quality of his bowl results. Of course, he left competent leaders in place who would honor the Michigan Football Tradition and carry it on for as long as they could.

When Bo left the sidelines in January 1990, his coaching "legend" was clearly established. Now, it was time to begin work on his true "legacy." This was just the start of another twenty-one-year era of Bo's impact, but this time it would be off the field. Bo didn't set out to be the greatest ambassador in the history of the University of Michigan, but that's exactly what happened.

In addition to winning a record number of games at Michigan, Bo left his mark on Michigan Football in many other areas. Some of them were little things and others were big things. However, all of them combined to create Bo's incredible legacy that enhanced the Michigan Football Tradition and built a solid foundation for those who followed him. Bo did everything for a reason. He was always looking for a way to improve his program, build player morale and foster loyalty amongst his players. Here is a short summary of some of Bo's initiatives and the many things that continue to be part of the Michigan Football Tradition.

Those Who Stay Will Be Champions.

Bo's famous sign had a humble beginning that I already described in Chapter 5. The amazing thing about the sign was that Bo had not won a single game as a head coach in the Big Ten when it was hung in Yost Field House in 1969. Here was this "rookie" coach "promising" his players, seniors included, that they would be champions if they survived that first grueling season in 1969. This was one of the boldest things a college football coach has ever done, but oh how it worked! Now, forty-five years later, this phrase is etched in the walls of Schembechler Hall. Bo was able to fulfill his promise to every player who played for him and so was Gary Moeller. Lloyd Carr was able to do it for ten of his thirteen recruiting classes. It is the standard that all Michigan Football coaches and players strive to achieve. Any questions?

Helmet Stickers.

Bo used the power of these little footballs to reward his players for making big plays and contributing to the success of the team. (Note – Lloyd Carr discontinued the tradition during his tenure because he felt they took away from the team focus and cluttered the classic look of Michigan's legendary helmets.) Jim Harbaugh enjoyed that tradition as a player. Now, Head Coach Harbaugh uses stickers to accomplish the same results that Bo did.

Team Photographs.

Prior to his arrival, only the lettermen sat for the "official" team picture. Bo felt that if a guy made it through Spring and Fall Drills he should have his photo taken as a member of the team. Bo's version of the "team picture", with over 100 players and coaches, continues to this day.

Bowl Game Travel.

When Bo was told that he could not take his entire team to a bowl game he said he wouldn't take anybody. He pointed out that the entire band and all the cheerleaders went to a bowl game so his whole team needed to attend as well. Pretty hard to argue that one!

Varsity Letters.

Again, this was another big deal for Bo. He didn't believe "playing time" should determine who received a letter and who did not. Bo knew that the program he wanted to run demanded that he have a lot of players because his practices were so physical. With the limitations on scholarships and the real possibility of injuries, Coach Schembechler knew that he had to have a lot of guys on his squad. He wanted all the walk-ons he could get on the practice field because he knew they were critical to Michigan's success on Game Day. If you came to the practices and busted your butt for Bo you probably got a letter and that's the way it should be!

The Greatest Attendance Streak in College Football History.

The Ninety-sixth team in the History of Michigan Football played seven home games and four of them were in front of 100,000 people or more. On October 25, 1975, a Homecoming Crowd of 93,857 witnessed a blowout victory (55-7) over the Indiana Hoosiers. This was the last time the Wolverines played in front of a home crowd of less than six figures. A crowd of 102,415 people showed up on November 8, 1975 to savor a shutout victory (28-0) over Purdue. This was the start of an attendance streak that is unequaled in college football history. At the end of the 2017 season, "The Streak" stands at 279 games with no end in sight. Yes, Don Canham had a big hand in this streak as well, but it would not have happened if Bo and his magnificent players had not won a ton of games in the early 1970s!

Bowl Game Opportunities.

Michigan, along with the rest of the Big Ten Conference, had limited opportunities to go to post-season bowl games prior to 1976. The conference had an agreement with the Rose Bowl, but the archaic "No-Repeat Rule" made it impossible for a team to go two years in a row. This rule created lots of "drama" over the years, but it all came to a boiling point in 1973 when the Big Ten's Athletic Directors voted to send ohio state after the infamous 10-10 tie between the Wolverines and the buckeyes. Bo went crazy, said some critical things to the press that implied wrong doing and undue influence. He was reprimanded by Big Ten Commissioner Wayne Duke for his "unsportsmanlike actions." Eventually, Bo's remarks caused enough of a stir that the conference changed the policy to allow teams to go to other bowl games besides the Rose Bowl. It turned out to be a great decision, especially financially, for the Big Ten Conference and Michigan. However, as Bo always said, "It was a helluva price to pay."

Strength Coach.

This was a practical decision to keep up with the times and to allow his players to be safer and more competitive on the field. It was a critical hire for Bo because the strength coach (and his staff) is the only "coach" who can be in contact with players on a year-round basis. Coach Schembechler hired the perfect guy, Mike Gittleson, who served Bo, his players and Michigan for over thirty years! In his book, *Tradition,* Schembechler said, "When it comes to strength and conditioning, Mike Gittleson is the best."

Weight Training Facilities.

This seems like a no-brainer, but it didn't happen at Michigan until Bo made it happen. Bo knew that the other top schools were building impressive weight training facilities for their football programs. Since he convinced Don Canham to hire a coach/staff to do it, it was only logical that he would ask for the tools and equipment to get this important work done! The weight training facilities have evolved over the years. Michigan continues to invest in the facilities, equipment and coaching that affords every player the opportunity to prepare to compete at the elite level of college football. (Note-Michigan's Board of Regents approved more improvements to Schembechler Hall so that the Wolverines can continue to be on the cutting-edge of player development.)

The Team, The Team, The Team.

A short locker room speech delivered before his team in 1983 became another mantra for Bo's version of Michigan Football. It guides the thoughts and actions of Michigan's Football players nearly five decades later. Got it?

Michigan Man Persona.

Bo fired the "coaching cliché" heard round the college sports world when he terminated Head Basketball Coach Bill Frieder just prior to the start of the NCAA Basketball Championship

Tournament in March 1989. Frieder had two degrees from Michigan while his interim replacement, Steve Fischer, held a degree from Illinois State University. This was confusing to a lot of people, but not to Bo. Athletic Director Schembechler didn't like the way that Frieder handled his sneaky departure to Arizona State University. Instead of accepting Frieder's offer to coach the team before he left town - Bo fired him!

Bo's definition of a "Michigan Man" did not focus solely on possessing a degree from the famous academic institution. Instead, it was defined by loyalty and trust and fidelity to the University and the people and programs you represented. So, a lot of people began to think differently about what a "Michigan Man" really was after this incident.

The Center of Champions (aka Schembechler Hall).

Bo's efforts to fix the "**Fourth F**," **F**acilities - dated back to his first season at Michigan when conditioning drills were held in Yost Field House. There wasn't a lot of weight training equipment and locker rooms were in short supply for coaches and players alike. In 1969, when one of his coaches complained that they had it better back at Miami of Ohio, Schembechler's response was memorable. He told the young coach something like "Fielding Yost might have hung his hat on that nail." So, instead of focusing on what Michigan didn't have, Schembechler pointed out that Michigan had a great tradition that no other school had and moved on. Bo knew that the facilities were pretty poor, but he wasn't going to let his coaches use them as an excuse. However, he also knew that opposing coaches had no problem pointing out such shortcomings to potential recruits so Bo knew that Michigan's practice facilities had to improve. Although he didn't lose any sleep over it, he advocated for better facilities for his coaches, players and the program in general. When Bo added Athletic Director to his title, he created a vision and a plan to build a first-class football facility that would be called "The Center of Champions." Bo, and former President Gerald R. Ford, spearheaded a fund-raising campaign that produced over thirteen million dollars. Michigan's Board of Regents opted to re-name the new facility "Schembechler Hall" just prior to a dedication ceremony in May 1992. Once again, Bo's vision left a positive and lasting impression on the Michigan Football Program – forever!

Note. Like Fielding H. Yost before him, Bo was intent on building something for the future that he might not personally enjoy. Fielding Yost retired from coaching so that he could focus on building his magnificent Michigan Stadium. Ironically, Yost never coached a single game in the stadium that he envisioned and built for the Michigan Football Ages. Bo also built something for "the next guy" named Gary Moeller and those who followed. Interestingly enough, Bo never occupied the Head Coaches' Office in the building that bears his name although he did have an office as Coach Emeritus until his death in 2006.

The Wolverine Magazine/Web Site.

Bo told longtime Sports Information Director and media marvel Bruce Madej that "We need a magazine that promotes Michigan Athletics, but mostly it has to be about football, football, football." Bo probably added a - "Got it?" to make sure Madej understand the "expectation." Once again, Bo knew that other schools had something like this and he wanted to make sure Michigan had the best sports magazine – period! Bruce Madej found Stu Coman and *The Wolverine* was created. As usual, the standards are high at Michigan so Coman and his staff must achieve a high level of excellence with their magazine, web page and blogs to keep all Die-Hard Wolverine Fans as well-informed as any in the country.

The Winningest Coach in Michigan Football History!

I had no plan to end this section on a "high note" when I first wrote it, but I would like to share some interesting data that I discovered while researching this book. Coach Schembechler's "Bowl Game" winning percentage of only .294 was the lowest of any Michigan coach as of 1989. Fielding Yost, on the other hand, was perfect, having won his only Rose Bowl appearance by a score of 49-0 over Stanford. It would have been interesting to see how Mr. Yost would have fared in ten to fifteen more games. Based on his track record, he probably would have won quite a few more bowl games. So, comparing Bo and the legendary Yost on bowl game success is a futile effort. However, things get a little more interesting when you look at how both men fared in their "regular season" bodies of work. Fielding H. "Hurry Up" Yost coached in a total of 203 regular season games and posted a record of 164 wins, 29 losses and 10 ties in those contests. Glenn E. "Bo" Schembechler led his team for 230 regular season games and finished with a total of 189 victories, 36 defeats and 13 ties. The following chart reveals how the numbers worked out for both Michigan Legends.

Regular Season Comparison – Yost and Bo

Coach	Games	W-L-T	B10 Titles	National Champs	Win %
Yost	203	164-29-10	10	6	.8325
Bo	230	189-36-5	13	0	.8326

Bo didn't win his first eleven games, nor did he go unbeaten in his first fifty-plus games, like Yost. What he did do was win at a very high rate for a very long time. Yost coached longer than Bo, but did not coach in as many games because of the Big Ten Conference schedule limits and other factors. When you look at the amazing numbers for both coaches, you see that Bo was better, in every category but national championships. The bottom line was that Bo could flat out coach, especially in the regular season. What happened to Bo's teams in December and January certainly mystified him and all the fans of Wolverine Nation. Once again, I believe that Bo's numbers gave Michigan Fans the "Greatest Era of Wolverine Football" based on the extensive number of wins, winning seasons, Big Ten Conference Championships, and everything else that Bo accomplished in Ann Arbor. I hope you learned something from my research into the amazing Michigan legacy of Glenn Edward "Bo" Schembechler.

ONE OF MY FAVORITE PICTURES OF COACH GLENN EDWARD "BO" SCHEMBECHLER

A FINAL ODE TO BO BY BARRY GALLAGHER

A Final Ode to Bo

Glenn Edward Schembechler, the man who we called "Bo"
Came to old Ann Arbor town a long, long time ago.
He came to coach the Wolverines, of legendary football fame
This tough, hard driving buckeye with the unpronounceable name!

People scoffed at AD Canham for his apparent oversight
Hiring a "Little Woody" to coach, somehow just didn't seem right.
But, Schembechler proved his loyalty that very first coaching year
When his Wolverines ambushed the buckeyes and knocked Woody on his ear!

In twenty-one years of coaching the fabled Maize and Blue
Bo accomplished everything that a football coach should do.
Big Ten titles rolled in, like cars off the assembly line
Thirteen of his twenty-one teams were champions starting in sixty-nine!

Bowl games became a habit for players and fans alike
The Wolverine faithful looked forward to their annual mid-winter hike.
Bo recruited outstanding players from places far and near
He coached forty All-Americans and had some new ones every year!

And if winning is your yardstick, then Bo was quite a man
His lofty winning percentage satisfied even the most ardent fan.
He toiled in the shadows of Crisler, Oosterbaan, Elliott and Yost
But, after all the years and games, twas Bo who won the most!

"The Team, The Team, The Team" was his famous battle cry
His players responded by thinking "We" instead of a selfish "I."
Defense and the running game were his famous bread and butter
Eventually, he let his quarterbacks throw the ball, but hated to watch it flutter!

His two hundred thirty-four wins placed him among the all-time best
Somehow, he survived the pressures and maintained his youthful zest.
Like a maestro leading his orchestra, he was a master of his craft
He excelled as a teacher and leader and loved to share a good laugh!

Ufer said "General Bo" was a great one, but he always said, "No Way!"
Maybe he was just a man with his whistle who was thankful for each new day.
He finished his career atop Michigan's all-time victory heap
And to every player who stayed with him – his promise he did keep!

THOSE WHO STAYED WERE CHAMPIONS!

BO'S TWENTY-ONE SEASONS AT MICHIGAN

Year	Overall	Big Ten	Place	AP Poll	UPI Poll
1969	8-3-0	6-1-0	1st-Tie	9th	8th
1970	9-1-0	6-1-0	2nd-Tie	9th	7th
1971	11-1-0	8-0-0	1st Place	6th	7th
1972	10-1-0	7-1-0	1st-Tie	6th	6th
1973	10-0-1	7-0-1	1st-Tie	6th	6th
1974	10-1-0	7-1-0	1st-Tie	3rd	5th
1975	8-2-2	7-1-0	2nd Place	8th	8th
1976	10-2-0	7-1-0	1st-Tie	3rd	3rd
1977	10-2-0	7-1-0	1st-Tie	9th	8th
1978	10-2-0	7-1-0	1st-Tie	5th	5th
1979	8-4-0	6-2-0	3rd Place	18th	19th
1980	10-2-0	8-0-0	1st Place	4th	4th
1981	9-3-0	6-3-0	3rd-Tie	12th	12th
1982	8-4-0	8-1-0	1st Place	N/R	15th
1983	9-3-0	8-1-0	2nd Place	8th	9th
1984	6-6-0	5-4-0	6th-Tie	N/R	N/R
1985	10-1-1	6-1-1	2nd Place	2nd	2nd
1986	11-2-0	7-1-0	1st-Tie	8th	7th
1987	8-4-0	5-3-0	4th Place	19th	18th
1988	9-2-1	7-0-1	1st Place	4th	4th
1989	10-2-0	8-0-0	1st Place	7th	8th
TOTALS	**194-48-5**	**143-24-3**	**13-1st Place**	-	-

BO'S MICHIGAN COACHING TIMELINE

Date	Event/Game	Location	Result	Milestone (s)
12/28/68	Meeting	Ann Arbor, MI	Bo Hired	1st Press Conference (12/28/68)
09/20/69	Vanderbilt	Ann Arbor, MI	Won (42-14)	1st Win/1st Home Win
10/11/69	Purdue	Ann Arbor, MI	Won (31-20)	1st Big Ten Win
10/25/69	Minnesota	Minneapolis, MN	Won (35-9)	1st Road Win/Big Ten Road Win
11/01/69	Wisconsin	Ann Arbor, MI	Won (35-7)	1st of 21 straight Homecoming wins
11/08/69	Illinois	Champaign, IL	Won (57-0)	1st of 54 career UM shutouts
11/22/69	ohio state	Ann Arbor, MI	Win (22-14)	1st Win over #1 team/1st Co-Champs
01/01/70	Rose Bowl	Pasadena, CA	Lost (3-10)	1st Heart Attack/1st Bowl Loss
11/20/71	ohio state	Ann Arbor, MI	Won (10-7)	1st B10 Champs/1st 8-0-0 season
11/08/75	Purdue	Ann Arbor, MI	Won (28-0)	1st game of 100k attendance streak
09/25/76	Navy	Ann Arbor, MI	Won (70-14)	Most points in UM Stadium history
10/09/76	MSU	Ann Arbor, MI	Won (42-10)	50th Big Ten win
10/06/79	MSU	East Lansing, MI	Won (21-7)	100th UM win
11/03/79	Wisconsin	Madison, WI	Won (54-0)	75th Big Ten win
01/01/81	Washington	Pasadena, CA	Won (23-6)	1st bowl win
11/07/81	Illinois	Ann Arbor, MI	Won (70-21)	Most points vs B10 team at UM
01/15/82	Texas A&M	Ann Arbor, MI	Bo Stays	Loyalty trumps $3 million
11/13/82	Purdue	Ann Arbor, MI	Won (52-21)	Clinched 10th B10 championship
10/08/83	MSU	East Lansing, MI	Won (42-0)	100th Big Ten win
10/05/85	Wisconsin	Ann Arbor, MI	Won (33-6)	150th Michigan win
10/11/86	MSU	Ann Arbor, MI	Won (27-6)	100th win in UM Stadium
11/22/86	ohio state	Columbus, OH	Won (26-24)	166th Michigan win (Record)
11/18/89	Minnesota	Minneapolis, MN	Won (49-15)	Last road win
11/25/89	ohio state	Columbus, OH	Won (28-18)	Last win-#194 @ UM-New record
01/01/90	USC	Pasadena, CA	Lost (10-17)	Last game

BO'S COACHING HONORS TIMELINE

Year	Coaching Award/Honor or Induction
1969	Bo named CFB National Coach of the Year
1972	Bo inducted into Miami (Ohio) Hall of Fame
1973	Bo becomes first man to be named Big Ten Coach of the Year
1976	Bo becomes first man to be named twice as Big Ten Coach of the Year
1980	Bo becomes first man to be named 3x Big Ten Coach of the Year
1985	Bo becomes first man to be named 4x Big Ten Coach of the Year
1986	Bo wins #166 at UM to pass Fielding Yost as winningest coach in UM Football History
1989	Bo inducted into the State of Michigan Sports Hall of Fame
1991	Michigan's new Center of Champions building dedicated & renamed Schembechler Hall
1992	Bo inducted in the University of Michigan Hall of Honor
1993	Bo inducted into the Rose Bowl Hall of Fame
1993	Bo inducted into the National Football Foundation Hall of Fame
1993	Bo inducted into the College Football Hall of Fame
1998	Bo earns Duffy Daugherty Memorial Award for a lifetime of achievement/contributions to college football.
2011	Big Ten Coach of the Year Award named after Bo and Woody – the first two men to win the award
2014	Bo's statue dedicated just outside Schembechler Hall.

A CLOSER LOOK AT BO AND COLLEGE FOOTBALL'S BEST COACHES

Rank	Name (Last, First)	*Years	Won-Lost-Tied	Win %	**Win/Year	***N/Cs
1st	Paterno, Joe	46	409-136-3	.750	8.89	2
2nd	Bowden, Bobby	44	377-129-4	.743	8.56	2
3rd	Stagg, Amos A.	57	329-190-35	.630	5.77	2
4th	Bryant, Paul	38	323-85-17	.780	8.50	6
5th	Warner, Glenn	44	319-106-32	.730	7.25	4
6th	Beamer, Frank	35	280-143-4	.660	8.00	0
7th	Edwards, LaVell	29	257-101-3	.716	8.86	1
8th	Osborne, Tom	25	255-49-3	.835	10.2	3
9th	Holtz, Lou	33	249-132-7	.650	7.54	1
10th	Brown, Mack	30	244-122-0	.667	8.13	1
11th	Hayes, Woody	33	238-72-10	.760	7.21	5
12th	Schembechler, Bo	27	234-65-8	.775	8.67	0

*Number of years as a Head Football Coach at a major college football program.

**Average wins per season

***National Championships

Note- This is an interesting chart because it shows that Bo is 12th in overall wins after 27 years of coaching. No, he didn't win any "mythical" national championships like most of the men on this impressive list. However, he has the third best winning percentage behind Tom Osborne and Bear Bryant. Bo also averaged 8.67 wins per season which puts him in fourth place behind Osborne, Joe Paterno and LaVelle Edwards. I'll say it again – Bo could flat out coach! Any questions?

BO'S 15 BIGGEST WINS (CHRONOLOGICAL ORDER)

Date	Location	UM vs Opponent	Score	Remarks, Notes or Comments
11/29/69	Home	#12 UM vs #1 osu	24-12	1st win over #1 and 1st B10 Co-Title
11/20/71	Home	#3 UM vs osu	10-7	1st B10 Championship (8-0-0)
11/18/72	Home	#3 UM vs Purdue	9-6	Lantry keeps UM unbeaten (10-0-0)
10/18/75	Home	#7 UM vs Northwestern	69-0	Bo's biggest win margin
11/20/76	Away	#4 UM vs #8 osu	22-0	Bo's 7X B10 title/1st osu shutout
10/27/79	Home	#10 UM vs Indiana	27-21	Wangler + Carter = HC winner!
01/01/81	Away	#5 UM vs #16 U-Wash.	23-6	Bo's 1st Bowl win/1st Rose Win
09/19/81	Home	#11 UM vs #1 ND	25-7	2nd win over #1 team
10/22/83	Home	#10 UM vs #12 Iowa	16-13	Bergeron wins it!
09/08/84	Home	#14 UM vs #1 Miami (FL)	22-14	3rd & last win over #1 team
01/01/86	Away	#5 UM vs #8 Nebraska	27-23	Fiesta Bowl win = #2 final ranking
10/18/86	Home	#4 UM vs #8 Iowa	20-17	Gillette gives UM 6-0 start
11/22/86	Away	#6 UM vs #7 osu	26-24	Bo wins #166 to pass Yost
01/02/89	Away	#11 UM vs #5 USC	22-14	Bo's last bowl win
11/25/89	Home	#3 UM vs #20 osu	28-18	Bo's last UM win #194

THOSE WHO STAYED WERE CHAMPIONS*
(JUST LIKE BO PROMISED!)

Frosh	Soph	Junior	Senior	5th Senior	# Big Ten Titles``
1966	1967	1968	**1969**	1970	1
1967	1968	**1969**	1970	**1971**	1-2
1968	**1969**	1970	**1971**	1972	2-3
1969	1970	**1971**	1972	1973	3-4
1970	**1971**	1972	1973	**1974**	3-4
1971	**1972**	**1973**	**1974**	1975	4
1972	**1973**	**1974**	1975	**1976**	3-4
1973	**1974**	1975	**1976**	**1977**	3-4
1974	1975	**1976**	**1977**	**1978**	3-4
1975	**1976**	**1977**	**1978**	1979	3
1976	**1977**	**1978**	1979	**1980**	3-4
1977	**1978**	1979	**1980**	1981	3
1978	1979	**1980**	1981	**1982**	2-3
1979	**1980**	1981	**1982**	1983	2
1980	1981	**1982**	1983	1984	2
1981	**1982**	1983	1984	1985	1
1982	1983	1984	1985	**1986**	1-2
1983	1984	1985	**1986**	1987	1
1984	1985	**1986**	1987	**1988**	1-2
1985	**1986**	1987	**1988**	**1989**	2-3
1986	1987	**1988**	**1989**	**1990**	3-4
1987	**1988**	**1989**	**1990**	**1991**	3-4
1988	**1989**	**1990**	**1991**	**1992**	4-5
1989	**1990**	**1991**	**1992**	1993	4

*Bold = A Big Ten Championship or Co-Championship

ONE MORE LOOK AT BO AND THE BIG TEN

Team	Overall	Big Win	Big Loss	Shut Outs	No Score	*Most	**Fewest
Illinois	19-1-1	57-0	6-16	4	0	70	3
Indiana	16-1-0	61-7	10-14	2	0	61	10
Iowa	13-3-1	63-7	0-26	2	1	63	0
MSU	17-4-0	42-0	7-19	4	0	42	7
Minnesota	19-2-0	49-0	0-16	3	1	58	0
NW	14-0-0	69-0	N/A	5	0	69	7
OSU	11-9-1	22-0	6-21	1	0	34	6
Purdue	16-3-0	51-0	21-24	4	0	52	14
Wisconsin	18-1-0	56-0	14-21	6	0	62	14

*Most points scored against each Big Ten opponent.

**Fewest points scored against each Big Ten opponent.

ABOUT THE AUTHOR

BARRY GALLAGHER WAS born in Pontiac, Michigan and spent most of his first thirty years living and working in southeastern Michigan. From 1973 to 1983 he worked as a teacher, coach and school administrator and also served in the U. S. Army Reserve. In 1983, he went on active duty served in various positions as a Military Police Office and Human Resources Officer and retired as a Colonel in 2003. He is very happily married, the father of five children and grandfather to twelve of his favorite children in the whole world. He enjoys spending time with his family, reading, writing, public speaking and following his favorite professional and college sports teams. In addition to *Michigan Football's Most Important Era (2014)*, he also authored two other books, *The Secrets of Life Power (2008)* and *How to Get a Kick Out of Coaching Youth Soccer (1994)*. Gallagher (along with his son Marty) is part of the first, and only, father-son team to write books about Michigan Football. Marty's book, *The Story of the Heisman and the Michigan Man,* was published in 2008. They plan to collaborate on other books about Wolverine Football in the future.

MAJOR BARRY GALLAGHER WITH GLENN E. "BO" SCHEMBECHLER IN BO'S OFFICE IN 1987.

PHOTOGRAPH PERMISSIONS AND DOCUMENTATION

ONCE AGAIN, THANK you to the Bentley Historical Library at The University of Michigan for permission to use the eight pictures listed below. The rest of the photographs in this book came from the Gallagher Family collection.

Book Page	BHL #	Description of Photograph
Cover	N/A	Gallagher Family Collection
Page xvii	N/A	From One Glenn E. to Another
Page 23	BL008655	Bo and Bump 1968
Page 53	BL013010	Bo and Jim Mandich 1969
Page 60	BL013712	Bo with Becker and Muransky 1981
Page 75	BL 017973	Classic Bo Pose
Page 112	BL 008816	Bo Surrounded in a "Huddle"
Page 118	BL 008608	Bo and Canham with Picture
Page 134	BL 008853	Bo Leads Team at Media Day
Page 143	HS 6526	Bo near the end of his career
Page 161	N/A	Major Gallagher and Bo

ACKNOWLEDGEMENTS

THERE ARE ALWAYS a large number of people to thank when a book is published. This book is no exception. I will start with the most important person in my life, my wife Carol. I could not have written this book without her constant love and support. She is the most understanding, and loving, person I know. I am so fortunate to have shared the best portion of my life with this amazing woman. She always keeps me grounded and has always supported me in my work. Thank you, my darling!

Second, I am grateful to all five of our children for their love and support over the years. Even though I have fathered Army Mules, Spartans, Broncos, and Xavier Musketeers, they still love me even though I love the Michigan Wolverines! Thank you, children, times five!

Third, I want to thank Mike Koenigs, Barry Schimmel, and John McCabe for their help in bringing this book to life and helping me make it a best seller! I could not have done it without their support. Thank you, gentlemen, for all your hard work!

Fourth, I am so grateful to the Bentley Historical Library at The University of Michigan. The Bentley Library is an amazing repository of the history of The University of Michigan. The incredible collection of football records, pictures and documents helped me greatly in researching and writing his book. Greg Kinney has helped me at every turn and is truly deserving of a "Special" thanks. Thanks Greg and to everyone at the BHL – you are absolutely the best at what you do!

Fifth, I always take time to thank my high school Creative Writing teacher, Mr. Richard Hill. He taught me some important things about writing that I still practice today. Most importantly, he instilled a passion for writing that I carry with me over fifty-years later! Mr. Hill was also a die-hard Michigan Wolverine Fan and graduate of The University of Michigan. Thank you, Mr. Hill!

Sixth, I will always be grateful to Bo Schembechler for all the time and support he gave me from 1985 to 1989. He helped me take care of a friend with a special picture that turned out to be an amazing retirement gift. Bo supported my efforts to raise scholarship funds with a poem that I wrote about the famous coach. Finally, Coach Schembechler even offered to help my oldest son earn an appointment to the United States Military Academy at West Point. However, when he found out that Mike got in on his own, Coach Schembechler congratulated him! I am thankful to Coach Schembechler and wish I would have finished this book before he died. I think he would have like it!

Seventh, I am so thankful to Glenn Doughty for the amazing Foreword that he wrote. He was there right from the start and saw Bo in action from Day One! His words take the reader back to a special time in Michigan Football History. Thank you, Glenn for being a friend and a great Michigan Man – the kind of person that Bo was always so proud of! Go Blue!

Finally, thank you to Mill City Press and Salem Author Services for all their help in getting this project completed. I want to offer a special "Thank You" to my project coordinator, Jennifer Toledo, for all of her patience and professionalism. Thank you Jennifer!